May Christ always be at the center.

COMPETE INSIDE

100 Reflections to Help You
Become the Complete Athlete

THOMAS WURTZ

Foreword by Mike Sweeney

WESTBOW®
PRESS
A DIVISION OF THOMAS NELSON
& ZONDERVAN

"Nihil Obstat: Mr. Derek Barr, M.B.T.
Censor Deputatus
Imprimatur: +Most Reverend Samuel J. Aquilla, S.T.L.
Archbishop of Denver,
Denver, Colorado, USA
March 24, 2015

Scripture from The Revised Standard Version of the Bible: Catholic Edition, copyright © 1965, 1966 the Division of Christian Education of the National Council of the Churches of Christ in the United States of America. Used by permission. All rights reserved.

WestBow Press books may be ordered through booksellers or by contacting:

WestBow Press
A Division of Thomas Nelson & Zondervan
1663 Liberty Drive
Bloomington, IN 47403
www.westbowpress.com
1 (866) 928-1240

Because of the dynamic nature of the Internet, any web addresses or links contained in this book may have changed since publication and may no longer be valid. The views expressed in this work are solely those of the author and do not necessarily reflect the views of the publisher, and the publisher hereby disclaims any responsibility for them.

Any people depicted in stock imagery provided by Thinkstock are models, and such images are being used for illustrative purposes only. Certain stock imagery © Thinkstock.

ISBN: 978-1-4908-6839-4 (sc)
ISBN: 978-1-4908-6840-0 (hc)
ISBN: 978-1-4908-6838-7 (e)

Library of Congress Control Number: 2015901632

Print information available on the last page.

WestBow Press rev. date: 04/07/2015

Dedicated to Rocco and Cecilia, my amazing children who are teaching me daily and calling me to a higher standard.

CONTENTS

AN ATHLETE'S PRAYER

Heavenly Father,
As I compete, help me to seek your glory, with
a brotherly affection towards my opponent,
always striving to see you in them.
As I sweat and fight through pain, help me unite my
struggle to the suffering of your son on the cross.
If I win, allow it to be for your honor, in
your name, with a humble heart.
If I fail, let it be with dignity and a courageous spirit,
always willing to stand strong and compete again.
Make my desire for greatness firm, yet with
peace of mind know that my worth is always
found in you, in victory or defeat.
I ask this through Jesus Christ our Lord.
Amen.

FOREWORD

I earned over $70,000,000 in Major League Baseball while playing a game that I would have played for free! At the beginning of my professional career as a 17 year old boy 3000 miles away from home, I literally was almost playing for free and loved every second of it. Minor League Baseball is not the place to plan your 401k or Roth IRA's but instead receive a crash course on getting a PhD in baseball! If you fail the course, your dream is forever squashed. If you succeed, you live on for yet another day. In Rookie Ball, my paycheck told me I was clearing $6.45 a day, but I was learning at a rapid pace priceless daily lessons about hard work, dedication, perseverance and most importantly *my faith*!

While playing for the Gulf Coast Royals in Baseball City, Florida, our days were a monotonous grind. We were required to live in two level dormitories where young men from all over the world were randomly paired up in 12' x 12' white cinderblock walled rooms equipped with a desk, chair, bunk bed and sink. Breakfast was served promptly in the downstairs cafeteria from 6am-7am. Immediately following breakfast, we had to be in the locker room...no later than 7:30am. There we would get treatment from the trainers, lift weights and hit in the batting cages. All of this to be ready to be on the work line by 9am for a two hour morning practice. We would then take the half mile walk back to the cafeteria to eat lunch, which consisted of sandwiches and soup made of beef stock and last night's dinner to get fueled up for the games. We would then walk back to the baseball complex by noon and prepare for the games which started daily at 1pm. The metal bleachers were almost always empty at our games except for an occasional girlfriend, parent or agent who would sometimes fill a seat. The long games felt like they were played in hot, humid saunas and, wow, were they draining! After our grueling three-plus hour games, our days were not complete until we ran our wind sprints and completed our weight lifting. We would then stammer back like zombies to the dormitories for dinner at 5:30pm. We did this daily and, although this sounds more like boot camp at Fort Brag than the famous baseball movie *Bull Durham*, it was one of the greatest times in my life. The best part of this rigorous schedule was that on Sundays, we were given the day off! (Thank God!)

My first Sunday in professional baseball was going to be one I would never forget. As my teammates, who grew up everywhere from California to Georgia, Canada to Mexico and Puerto Rico to Dominican Republic, made plans to hit Daytona Beach or to go fishing, I thumbed through the yellow pages (before iPhones or the internet existed) to find the local church. I found St. Ann Catholic Church in Haines City, FL which was a 10.5 mile drive from our dormitory. I asked my teammate John "Bubba" Jacobs if he could give me a ride to church before he and the boys went to the beach if I put a few dollars of gas into his gas tank. He obliged and dropped me off at 8:55am at St Ann's. As I watched "Bubba" drive away in his sparkling new, cherry red, convertible Mustang GT, I wondered if I had made the right decision. It ended up being the best $4 I have ever spent.

Despite growing up close to Los Angeles and now sitting in a church just outside of Orlando, I felt right at home when I made the sign of the cross along with several hundred Christians as the celebration began. Although I was by far the youngest person in the church, I felt an incredible peace in my heart being in this House of God. As Mass ended, I watched as the grey and blue haired retiree's jumped in their Cadillacs and Buicks and drove away to breakfast. I watched until I looked up and noticed that the only two people left in the courtyard were me and the pastor. I ashamedly asked the Latin priest for a ride home, because I had no other means of transportation. He introduced himself as Fr. Domingo Gonzalez from Cuba and told me if I stayed for the 10:30am Spanish Mass, he would give me a ride home. I agreed because walking 10.5 miles down Highway 27 in the 98 degree south Florida heat sounded like a bad plan B. As the Spanish Mass concluded, I hopped into Fr. Domingo's blue Ford Escort Pony, and we putted away from the church. About half way home, we stopped at Golden Corral and had what tasted like the best meal of my life. After conversing about life and our common faith in Jesus over lunch, we proceeded to Baseball City. As Fr. Domingo dropped me off, he rolled down his window and said, "Michael, I will see you next Sunday at 8am." I replied, "Father, Mass is at nine." Fr. Domingo looked me in the eyes and with a big smile on his face responded, "Michael, I know. I will pick you up at eight o'clock and bring you back to the church where we will have breakfast together. You will attend the English Mass at 9am and the Spanish Mass at 10:30. We will then head to Golden

Corral afterwards for lunch." And he drove away. From that point forward, this became my weekly Sunday routine.

This season of life was one where I received a PhD in baseball but also one where my relationship with Jesus Christ became the most important part of my life. Fr. Domingo was an instrument (my mom says he was my Guardian Angel) that God used to keep me close to the heart of His Son during this time in my life where there was so much going on and there were so many distractions. Despite living out my childhood dreams of playing professional baseball, I couldn't wait for Sunday. I could not wait to squeeze into the little blue Ford and see this wonderful man of God who was leading me to Jesus. His encouragement led me to a daily desire to hustle back to the white cinderblock-walled dorm room after dinner to consume God's Word in my Bible, pray to our Lord and write letters to my loved ones in California.

Looking back, this time prepared me physically, mentally and spiritually to be the very best person and athlete I could be. Without Fr. Domingo and my intimate relationship with Jesus, I know I never would have achieved my dream of making it to the Big Leagues. Many men were bigger, stronger, faster and more talented than I was, but I had something they didn't: a *faith* in Jesus Christ that I lived out. Fr. Domingo encouraged me to be the man God wanted me to be – healthy body plus healthy mind plus healthy soul equals *a complete athlete!* This gave me the foundation and mindset to be my very best both on and off the field.

My dear friend and brother in Christ, Thomas Wurtz, has orchestrated a brilliant set of reflections specifically designed for athletes who want to be their very best, both on and off the playing field. I was blessed in my 16 year Major League Baseball career to play in 5 Major League Baseball All Star Games, hit home runs in front of 50,000 screaming fans and even pull off a straight steal of home against the New York Yankees. These were amazing feats and moments I will cherish forever, but they would have been impossible had it not been for my time in Florida.

As I devoured the 100 reflections of *Compete Inside,* I wish only one thing…that Thomas would have released this incredible book years ago, so that I could have read it daily in the bunk bed of that white cinderblock-walled dorm room in Baseball City, FL. It would have been an incredible gift to me at that time in my life. May this book be a tool that will help you become *the complete athlete* and child of God our Lord desires you to be.

This treasure, *Compete Inside*, will help bring you and your *faith* from rags to riches!!! Enjoy the run…

Mike Sweeney
December 2014

Mike is a former Major League Baseball standout where he was blessed to play for sixteen years. He was celebrated as an MLB All-Star five of those years with the Kansas City Royals. He was a career .297 hitter and holds the Royals record with 144 RBIs during the 2000 season, and narrowly missed the American League batting title when he hit .340 in 2002. He has served as a studio analyst for MLB Network and currently is back with the Royals in the front office. He was also selected as a member of the Kansas City Royals Hall of Fame.

Mike is the founder of Catholic Baseball Camps and the Mike and Shara Sweeney Foundation. He and his wife Shara have four children.

INTRODUCTION

Athletes:

You are busy, stressed, and have a lot expected of you. You possess astonishing motivation, extreme talent and are familiar with success. Your busy life, filled with these intense expectations, sometimes makes it difficult to keep things in the proper balance.

This book exists to aid each of you in becoming more of whom you were originally designed to be – a spectacular soul capable of remarkable accomplishments. Each of the one hundred reflections was written for you - from an upper classman in high school to the professional. They were written in first person with the hope that the concepts and challenges can be digested with ease, processed in a flash and relevant without question.

My hope, as the author, is that you work, with a slow pace, through each reflection, internalize the petition, pray through the Scripture and answer the reflection questions. For those of you who are just starting your walk with the Lord, I encourage you to make this journey with a mentor that can help you apply each concept, relate the Scripture and best determine the answers to the questions.

Self-knowledge serves a large part of improving as an athlete – just think of the film room. In our faith, self-knowledge is equally significant. These reflections are geared to help you discover more about yourself so that God can do even more with you.

The reflections can be read in any order, as many times as necessary. Some of the concepts may resonate more deeply than others, but do your best to enter into each one.

As you continue on your path as a Christian athlete, you may want to revisit these reflections every year or two. Each stage of our life gives us a different perspective with new experiences, and because of this you will gain something unique when you look at these reflections again.

Thank you for your desire to be a better athlete and Christian. If you persevere, you will make the world around you a better place.

ONE

My Identity

How I identify myself is powerful. It controls when I feel good. It controls when I don't.

This ability to sway my disposition is likely because I identify myself with things beyond my control. I see myself as an athlete, as a bright student, as a stud, as a beauty queen. I see myself and my worth based on the talents and skills I seem to possess. As they shine, my self-perception shines. As they wane, so does the worth I feel towards myself. It could be after I have failed or during a long struggle. It might be in the middle of a slump or a tough critique by some fans. My day can be like a roller coaster when I don't feel like I am worth anything.

I must remind myself that I am more than the things that make me stand out from the crowd. I am more than what I do and the accomplishments I have achieved. I am priceless in the eyes of my heavenly Father. His love for me is perfect. I am his child. No matter how often I fail, he will always love me and cast his mercy upon me. I must identify myself in this unchanging reality.

Thank you Father for your love for me that never fades. Remind me of my real identity when I seem to forget, and forget I will.

"So God created man in his own image, in the image of God he created him; male and female he created them." Gen 1:27

"For all who are led by the Spirit of God are sons of God. For you did not receive the spirit of slavery to fall back into fear, but you have received the spirit of sonship. When we cry, 'Abba! Father!' it is the Spirit himself bearing witness with our spirit that we are children of God..." Romans 8:14-16

What successes and failures seem to have the biggest impact on me? Which of my activities, abilities, and traits do I identify myself with the most? What is one tangible thing I can do to remind myself that I am a child of God?

Trusting Me

I seem to think through a lot of scenarios, a lot of "what ifs". In the two seconds before I shoot, swing, run, or jump, my mind seems to ask a million questions and create a thousand outcomes. To say the least, it is very distracting.

This distraction causes a lot of anxiety. I don't like all this uncertainty, especially knowing so many negative results could occur. What would my dad, my girlfriend, my boyfriend, my buddies, my coach, or my team think? If I miss, I might not play next game. It is amazing how easily I can doubt myself and my abilities. That doesn't sit well. I am overthinking things.

I need to trust my ability. I need to trust the effort and preparation I put in.

Lord, I need to trust you. You have my back, win or lose. Thank you for your unending support of me.

> "Look at the birds of the air: they neither sow nor reap nor gather into barns, and yet your heavenly Father feeds them. Are you not of more value than they? And which of you by being anxious can add one cubit to his span of life? And why are you anxious about clothing? Consider the lilies of the field, how they grow; they neither toil nor spin; yet I tell you, even Solomon in all his glory was not clothed like one of these. But if God so clothes the grass of the field, which today is alive and tomorrow is thrown into the oven, will he not much more clothe you, O you of little faith? Therefore do not be anxious, saying, 'What shall we eat?' or 'What shall we drink?' or 'What shall we wear?' For the Gentiles seek all these things; and your heavenly Father knows that you need them all. But seek first his kingdom and his righteousness, and all these things shall be yours as well. Therefore do not be anxious about tomorrow, for tomorrow will be anxious for itself. Let the day's own trouble be sufficient for the day." Matthew 6:26-34

Do I trust that God is faithful and wants the very best for me? How do I act counter to this reality? In which areas of my life do I need to trust more in the Lord? How can I improve self-trust in my athletic ability?

Every Day

What is my motivation to show up every day? Why should I? Is it for my own recognition and glory? For the scholarship? For my image?

Centuries ago people spent decades building beautiful churches. They gave fully of themselves and often died before the church was ever finished. Their motivation was God. They wanted to give him something back. They wanted to serve him and bring him glory.

As an athlete, I have been given so much by him. Everything actually. If I let him be my motivation, then nothing else will matter. The fans *really* don't matter. My success or failure *really* doesn't matter. I can give everything for him who gave everything for me. That is the greatest of all motivations.

Lord, be my inspiration, my reason to compete. I can give everything back to you, as a prayer, as a sacrifice, and as an offering. That is awesome.

> "Beware of practicing your piety before men in order
> to be seen by them; for then you will have no reward
> from your Father who is in heaven." Matthew 6:1

> "Who is wise and understanding among you? By his good life let
> him show his works in the meekness of wisdom. But if you have
> bitter jealousy and selfish ambition in your hearts, do not boast
> and be false to the truth. This wisdom is not such as comes down
> from above, but is earthly, unspiritual, devilish. For where jealousy
> and selfish ambition exist, there will be disorder and every vile
> practice. But the wisdom from above is first pure, then peaceable,
> gentle, open to reason, full of mercy and good fruits, without
> uncertainty or insincerity. And the harvest of righteousness
> is sown in peace by those who make peace." James 3:13-18

What are the motivations that seem to surface the most in my life? Are there certain triggers like jealousy, anger, or selfishness that often become motivations? When is the best time to say a prayer and remind myself God is my motivation?

FOUR

An Opportunity

Failure is not an option.

But failure is a reality – in my own life anyway. I have failed a few times or at least not been perfect. This is tough, because I am afraid to fail and disappoint. I am supposed to succeed; that is what everyone expects. That is what I do – succeed.

They say failure should be an opportunity to grow, to learn, or to improve. Is that true or just what people that fail say? I want to be the best – to be perfect. Is there a problem with that?

Why am I afraid to fail? Is it my ego? Is it vanity? Am I putting too much worth into success? It is not possible to be perfect this side of heaven. I should not desire to fail but should be okay with it if I do. I should learn from it. It is an opportunity to get better – closer to excellence. Every time I don't achieve excellence, I need to get up, regroup, and try again. If I learn and move on, I will be better off. It will keep me humble – keep me from being deceived into thinking that I am perfect.

Lord, remove this fear from my life so that I may strive for even better things, for your glory always.

> "but he said to me, 'My grace is sufficient for you, for my power is made perfect in weakness.' I will all the more gladly boast of my weaknesses, that the power of Christ may rest upon me. For the sake of Christ, then, I am content with weakness, insults, hardships, persecutions and calamities; for when I am weak, then I am strong." 2 Corinthians 12:9-10

Revisit that question, why am I afraid to fail? What can I do this week to face that fear?

Living with Success

How do I handle success? I love it, I want it, and I won't settle for anything less. How do I let it affect me? Hmm, good question. Do I boast? Do I grow more and more arrogant? Do I let it shape my self-perception? Or do I let it create in me a heart of gratitude? Does it remind me how much I depend on the Lord for everything?

Success can easily become addictive. It can blind me to anything outside of myself and my pursuit of success. In the midst of achievement, it is important to remember where everything comes from – our Lord. He has given me every opportunity to run after success. Now I need to succeed in a way pleasing to him: to rejoice in his glory, to acknowledge his blessings and gifts, to stay humble. If I begin to make myself bigger and bigger inside my own head, I will have farther to fall.

Lord, keep me humble in my success, seeing your hand in it always. Thank you, Jesus.

> "For what will it profit a man, if he gains the whole world and forfeits his life…" Matthew 16:26

> "This book of the law shall not depart out of your mouth, but you shall meditate on it day and night, that you may be careful to do according to all that is written in it; for then you shall make your way prosperous, and then you shall have good success." Joshua 1:8

How do I usually act when I achieve success? How can I channel those moments so they bring glory to God?

Honor and Respect

"Show me the honor I deserve."

"Respect me."

"Earn their respect."

I have often thought through those three phrases above, and others just like it. How others perceive me is important to me. I want people to respect me, to honor me, and to give me the credit I deserve.

I know there are moments when that desire becomes overpowering. It becomes my primary motivation. I see it happen to my teammates as well, even in the coaches.

I need to behave as one that is worthy of respect. That should be my concern, since that is in my power to control. People can choose not to show me respect; they have that freedom. But I can make that choice extremely difficult for them by living in a way that is wholly respectable.

Lord, all that is good comes from you. Every ability I have is from you. Every good thing I do is because of your grace. Help me to be confident in this, and no matter what people think of me, continue to pursue truth, goodness, and above all seek to love at every moment.

"Finally, brethren, whatever is true, whatever is honorable, whatever is just, whatever is pure, whatever is lovely, whatever is gracious, if there is any excellence, if there is anything worthy of praise, think about these things. What you have learned and received and heard and seen in me, do; and the God of peace will be with you." Philippians 4:8-9

"Let love be genuine; hate what is evil, hold fast to what is good; love one another with brotherly affection; outdo one another in showing honor." Romans 12:9-10

When do I try too hard to be respected? How does that negatively affect my actions? What should I focus on instead to become someone worthy of respect?

Competitive Spirit

Aren't Christians supposed to turn the other cheek? That must not help them as competitors. Weakness doesn't produce winners.

Actually, Jesus didn't turn the other cheek. When he gets smacked by the guard while standing before the High Priest, he looks the guard square in the eyes and asks him, "If I have spoken wrongly, bear witness to the wrong; but if I have spoken rightly, why do you strike me?" (John 18:23). He doesn't back down and curl up like a weak animal – he just doesn't return violence for violence.

If I imitate Jesus, I can imitate his tenacity. He wasn't weak – neither should I be weak. I should compete ferociously, because in doing so, I am using everything God gave me to its fullest. In having competitive spirit, I am faithfully striving after my potential and avoiding mediocrity.

Lord, help me give everything I have on the field, because you have given me the ability to do so. Don't let me be lazy with my gifts and talents. Win or lose, help me always give the best effort of every athlete out there.

> "Whatever your task, work heartily, as serving the
> Lord and not men, knowing that from the Lord you
> will receive the inheritance as your reward; you are
> serving the Lord Christ." Colossians 3:23-24

Why would I worry that having a friendship with Jesus Christ is going to make me a weaker athlete? Where does this worry come from?

My Image

It dictates how I shop, what I wear, the music I listen to, or even how I talk. It is the persona I want to project, how I want people to see me. It is *my* image.

I am the life of every party, the most popular girl, the guy that can do everything well, the one with piercing insight into every problem, the mountain man, the girl that takes fifteen minutes to make herself look like it took fifteen seconds to get ready, or the athlete. If people don't pick up on my image, it bothers me. I put so much energy into creating it. Why do I do that? Did I lose my self-confidence? Am I trying to hide something about myself that I am not proud of?

This attachment to my image restricts my freedom. I am confined to activities that personify this image and can't be my true self.

I know I am loved by God; I should take comfort in that and relax. This is where I will find freedom – the freedom to think of others more than myself. The freedom to just be and listen to the voice of the Lord in every moment. I don't need to worry about projecting an image. If I seek to love people, and think less of myself, I will find more joy and peace.

Lord, you made me, and you love me. Help me to embrace my quirks and my charms. Thank you for me.

> "For by the grace given to me I bid every one among you not
> to think of himself more highly than he ought to think, but
> to think with sober judgment, each according to the measure
> of faith which God has assigned him. For as in one body we
> have many members, and all the members do not have the
> same function, so we, though many, are one body in Christ,
> and individually members of one another. Having gifts that
> differ according to the grace given to us..." Romans 12:3-6

What are the images I seek to project? In what ways might these images restrict me from acting more true to myself, in accordance with whom my Lord created me to be?

Facing the Unknown

It didn't happen how I thought. This week, this day, or this season – wow – just not what I was wanting. It is hard to surrender control over these things in my life, especially with those that are not tangible. When I am actually competing, I know exactly where I stand - my stats are right there for me. In the other areas of my life, there is so much uncertainty. This is hard.

What will happen during this injury, when that new recruit transfers, or if I don't get the start this week? So many questions with no answers. Again, this creates anxiety. I want to let go, but it is hard. It is hard to surrender control. It is hard to live with so many unknowns. The best I can do is to focus on what I can control.

Lord, help me to follow in Mary's example when the angel Gabriel appeared to her. She trusted so perfectly: "Let it be done to me according to your word" (Luke 1:38). There were so many things she didn't know, yet she trusted. Help me surrender like Mary did. I know so much peace will follow when I put my trust in you and let go.

> "For I know the plans I have for you, says the
> LORD, plans for welfare and not for evil, to give
> you a future and a hope." Jeremiah 29:11

> "May the God of hope fill you with all joy and peace
> in believing, so that by the power of the Holy Spirit
> you may abound in hope." Romans 15:13

Which areas of my life do I seek to control? How am I affected when decisions don't go the way I want them to go? What are ways I can slowly surrender these areas over to God?

True Humility

To see myself as I truly am - that is what it means to be humble.

If I am good at something, acknowledge that I am good at it. It is only arrogance if I boast about it or hold it over the heads of those who aren't as good.

If I struggle at something, recognize that I struggle at it. Accept it and work to get better.

When I see myself as I truly am, I can come before God with greater purity. I come before him more in line with the way that he sees me. There is less contradiction. There is more harmony. This allows his grace to work more effectively in my soul.

It is also great for me as an athlete to recognize my ability with clarity, because it allows me to see where I need to improve. Without humility, I will be blind to my weaknesses. I will restrict my ability to improve.

Lord, help me to see myself clearly - to see myself as you see me. Remove arrogance from my heart and mind, since it makes me blind.

"He leads the humble in what is right, and
teaches the humble his way." Psalm 25:9

"...for everyone who exalts himself will be humbled, but
he who humbles himself will be exalted." Luke 18:14

In what ways am I not seeing myself clearly? How am I deceiving myself? What aspects about myself do I need to come to grips with?

For God's Glory

"He must increase; I must decrease," are famous words of John the Baptist. If this was my attitude all the time, how much better things would be. Why shouldn't it always be about Jesus and his glory? This elevates my motivation. When you have a strong reason to do something, it usually helps you do it better. My reason is for the creator of everything.

I walk because of him. I breathe because of him. I can compete in this sport because of him. Yes, it should be about him - after all, from his perspective, it is all about me. He gave his life for me. I have a tremendous opportunity to give everything back to him.

Lord, help me remember you at every moment of my life. Help me to compete for your greater glory.

> "Let your light so shine before men, that they
> may see your good works and give glory to your
> Father who is in heaven." Matthew 5:16

> "So, whether you eat or drink, or whatever you do,
> do all to the glory of God." 1 Corinthians 10:31

What is something on the practice field that can be my constant reminder of the Lord? Which habits can I start to develop during practice and games that can remind me of why I compete? What other actions in my life can I do with God's glory in mind?

TWELVE

Power Under Control

Jesus says, "the meek shall inherit the earth" (cf. Matthew 5:5). Not sure what that means, but it seems that the meek shall lose the game...

When I hear meekness, I think weakness. It doesn't seem to jive with being an athlete. Perhaps I don't have the right understanding of meekness.

Meekness means humbly patient or docile, as under provocation from others (dictionary.com). Interesting. The Christian understanding of meekness is a virtue (strength) that helps one control anger. Hmm. I can get angry easily while competing. Anger usually doesn't help me win. It usually makes me distracted from the task at hand. It takes me out of the present moment. I lose focus. Meekness can help me channel that emotion towards mental awareness and concentration. Meekness doesn't sound as bad anymore.

I have changed my mind. Meekness equals power under control. What a great trait to have.

Lord, keep me from flying off the handle. Allow me to channel my aggression towards a good. Help me stay focused.

> "Take my yoke upon your shoulders and learn from me; for I am gentle and lowly in heart, and you will find rest for your souls. For my yoke is easy, and my burden light." Matthew 11:29-30

> "A fool gives full vent to his anger, but a wise man quietly holds it back." Proverbs 29:11

> "Know this, my beloved brethren. Let every man be quick to hear, slow to speak, slow to anger, for the anger of man does not work the righteousness of God. Therefore put away all filthiness and rank growth of wickedness and receive with meekness the implanted word, which is able to save your souls." James 1:19-21

When am I most likely to burst out in anger? What mechanisms have I put in place to maintain calm? How can I practice the virtue of meekness?

My Desire for Fame

To be famous is to be talked about by lots of people, especially because of noteworthy accomplishments.

This is tempting. It is often part of my incentive – to be acknowledged and known. You can see my picture and bio on the website. I am a public figure. Fame, to some degree or another, comes with the territory. And I like it.

Ok, I shouldn't like it so much. It shouldn't be a reason I compete. Why not? Because it makes me focus on myself. This adds negative pressures, which in turn can become anxieties. And so goes a downhill spiral. Beyond that, playing for myself is never the right reason. It might be in vogue to be concerned with "number one", but that isn't the Christian way. It is always about *other*. That is how I am made. That is how I find fulfillment.

Lord, help me respond to your invitation to love my neighbor as myself. I don't want it to be all about me.

> "This is my commandment, that you love one another as
> I have loved you. Greater love has no man than this, that
> a man lay down his life for his friends." John 15:12-13

> "It shall not be so among you; but whoever would be great
> among you must be your servant, and whoever would
> be first among you must be your slave; even as the Son
> of man came not to be served but to serve, and to give
> his life as a ransom for many." Matthew 20:26-28

Who in my life have I been purposely avoiding? How can I reach out and show them love and redirect the attention from me to someone else?

FOURTEEN
Loving Despite the Fear

"Be not afraid" is mentioned in the Bible dozens of times. God knew how easily we would be afraid – afraid to trust, to surrender, and to give unconditionally.

It is hard. I have been hurt by people in the past: betrayed, rejected, and laughed at. There is so much suffering, in my life and around me, that I am afraid. I am afraid to be hurt again. I am afraid that giving of myself in love and service will only bring me more pain. I am afraid to be vulnerable.

I have heard that when I love, I will truly find myself and lasting joy. I want to act against my fears to see if this is true. God is love, so it makes perfect sense that in giving love we are brought closer to God and thus find joy. I must act with courage and face these fears. I think it is worth the risk.

Lord, give me the strength to lay my life down at every moment of every day. Help me to love despite my fear.

"Greater love has no man than this, that a man lay
down his life for his friends." John 15:13

"If the world hates you, know that it has hated me before it
hated you. If you were of the world, the world would love its
own; but because you are not of the world, but I chose you out
of the world, therefore the world hates you." John 15:18-19

As I look to the Lord's command to love one another, what causes the most fear? What about when I look at making Jesus Christ the center of my life? How can I face those fears?

Be Amateur Athletes

"When an athlete, even a professional one, cultivates this dimension of being an 'amateur', society benefits and that person strengthens the common good with the values of generosity, camaraderie and beauty." (Pope Francis' address to the delegations of the National Football Teams of Argentina and Italy, August 13th, 2013.)

Find the love of the game. Remember why I started playing in the first place – the joy I received from play. I need to be like a child again. When I play with that purity, I will embody the virtues the pope is talking about – generosity, camaraderie and beauty. I will be a witness to true brotherhood, to joy, and to love. I will be a witness to Jesus Christ.

I need to play for something beyond myself and recognize the responsibility I have to society that Pope Francis is speaking about. In purifying my intention for competition, I can more aptly serve the common good. I decrease my ego and become a servant leader. What a remarkable calling.

Lord, make me an instrument of peace. Help me to use the language of sport to unite, rather than tear apart. Help me to show generosity to my opponents and a camaraderie with teammates. In that, may I show others the beauty of a life well lived.

> "'All things are lawful,' but not all things are helpful. 'All things are lawful,' but not all things build up. Let no one seek his own good, but the good of his neighbor." 1 Corinthians 10:23-24

> "For we must all appear before the judgment seat of Christ, so that each one may receive good or evil, according to what he has done in the body." 2 Corinthians 5:10

What aspect of this reflection applies most in my life? How can I live the responsibility I have as an athlete to build up society?

SIXTEEN

A Servant

How can I worry about helping others when I am barely managing? I have so many demands on my time. I am expected to fulfill a lot of responsibilities, especially as an athlete. People need to learn to help themselves.

At the same time, I understand it is important to serve others – in the community, on my team, my peers, etc. Sometimes people need help, and I can offer that help. There must be a simple way I can serve that won't be too overwhelming.

There is. Even seemingly insignificant acts of service done with tremendous love will impact the world. I can do small bits of service to those in need, and if I have love in my heart when I do them, it will be pleasing in the Lord's eyes.

God, help me to follow your example and look upon those around me with great love in my heart. Help me to do small acts of service with love.

"For you were called to freedom, brethren; only do not use your freedom as an opportunity for the flesh, but through love be servants of one another. For the whole law is fulfilled in one word, 'You shall love your neighbor as yourself.'" Gal 5:13-14

"What does it profit, my brethren, if a man says he has faith but has not works? Can his faith save him? If a brother or sister is poorly clothed and in lack of daily food, and one of you says to them, 'Go in peace, be warmed and filled,' without giving them the things needed for the body, what does it profit? So faith by itself, if it has no works, is dead. But someone will say, 'You have faith and I have works.' Show me your faith apart from your works, and I by my works will show you my faith." James 2:14-18

What are opportunities I can serve a situation with love? When do these opportunities usually appear? What can I do to remind myself of these opportunities?

SEVENTEEN

Commitment

I chose to come here. I made a commitment. Some days it is very tempting to leave. The team, the coaches, the fans, the school, or the city can leave something to be desired at times. But I am grateful for this opportunity – one that few have. Being a part of this team is actually a blessing.

With that, I should give everything I have to this commitment. It is only fair if I am taking up a spot on this roster. It is my duty to be faithful to the expectations before me. Commit to them. Follow through. Stop feeling entitled.

Heavenly Father, you gave everything to me even though you didn't need to. Help me to be generous to what I have committed to. Give me the integrity to stay true to my word.

"Do not withhold good from those to whom it is due,
when it is in your power to do it." Proverbs 3:27

"Do nothing from selfishness or conceit, but in humility
count others better than yourselves." Philippians 2:3

In what ways might I be short-cutting the system? What expectations have I blown off? When do I keep from others what is due to them?

Witness Beyond Fear

When I really like something, I am usually eager to share it or talk about it with those around me. I do that all the time with good food and restaurants, with a good movie or book, with a great clip or show. It is so natural, and the joy just overflows.

It isn't that easy sharing Jesus with my teammates and those around me. Fear creeps in. I know I don't love Jesus as much as I should or want to, but it shouldn't be this hard to talk about something that is so important. It could make *the* difference for someone - for the rest of eternity.

I need to remember what it was like without you in my life, Lord. The thirst I had for something, and how nothing really ever quenched it no matter what I tried, who I dated, or what I consumed. I know so many people in my life are thirsting as well – for you.

I really have nothing to fear. I need to remind myself of this. I might get some rejection, maybe a snide comment or two. That is nothing compared to the joy I will receive seeing those around me, Lord willing, in heaven.

Lord, don't let me hide under a rock. Help me to be a living witness to your greatness and the offer of salvation you give us.

> "You are the light of the world. A city set on a hill cannot be hid. Nor do men light a lamp and put it under a bushel, but on a stand, and it gives light to all in the house. Let your light so shine before men, that they may see your good works and give glory to your Father who is in heaven." Matthew 5:14-16

> "Just so, I tell you, there will be more joy in heaven over one sinner who repents than over ninety-nine righteous persons who need no repentance." Luke 15:7

Who is my life do I need to share the story of how Jesus Christ changed my life. What is my game plan to do this?

NINETEEN

Leadership

Leadership is a term thrown around abundantly these days. I am supposed to be leading, as a leader. What does that look like? Am I supposed to be the most vocal, the player-coach, or the quiet leader? What if I am not good enough?

With all the struggles and mistakes in my life, I can still be an effective leader. This is hard to believe at times, but it is true. If I am attentive to the good of the team and those around me, and seek to serve those needs, I will be a leader.

I don't need to have a title, or get recognition for it. Leadership and service are intimately connected. When I serve, I am leading. When I am leading, I must be serving. This is the example of the King of kings himself.

Jesus, give me the heart of a servant-leader. Give me a heart like yours.

> "It shall not be so among you; but whoever would be great
> among you must be your servant, and whoever would
> be first among you must be your slave; even as the Son
> of man came not to be served but to serve, and to give
> his life as a ransom for many." Matthew 20:26-28

> "Have this mind among yourselves, which was in Christ
> Jesus, who, though he was in the form of God, did not
> count equality with God a thing to be grasped, but
> emptied himself, taking the form of a servant, being
> born in the likeness of men." Philippians 2:5-7

What attitudes or struggles get in the way and prevent me from having the attitude of a servant-leader? What can I replace those bad attitudes with?

A Higher Standard

There are a lot of people trying to speak into my life. I typically listen if they hold themselves to a high standard. When they "walk the walk," their words have more weight behind them. This moral authority in their life makes them great leaders worthy of following. They inspire me.

I desire this in my life – to strive for such a level of excellence, that when I seek to encourage others, they will likely listen. I think of people like Mother Teresa. When she challenged us to love, no one rolled their eyes; her life was a genuine witness to love. She "walked the walk." She set the standard in our modern world.

While I will likely not be perfect on or off the field, the effort and consistency in striving after the highest standard is the significant part. Trying and coming up short is not the same thing as hypocrisy.

Lord, help me to live a life of consistency in my words and actions. By your grace, make me a person exhibiting moral authority, especially as a disciple of Jesus Christ.

> "Woe to you, scribes and Pharisees, hypocrites! for
> you are like whitewashed tombs, which outwardly
> appear beautiful, but within they are full of dead men's
> bones and all uncleanness." Matthew 23:27

> "And he said to them, 'Well did Isaiah prophesy of you hypocrites,
> as it is written, "This people honors me with their lips, but their
> heart is far from me; in vain do they worship me, teaching as
> doctrines the precepts of men." You leave the commandment
> of God, and hold fast the tradition of men.'" Mark 7:6-8

What are the most glaring inconsistencies in my life? Where do I straddle the fence between being a follower of Jesus and drifting from him? How can I improve the standard that I hold myself to?

TWENTY-ONE

Heart of Envy

Envy – how easily it can pervade sports. I become sad or angry when someone else is successful. I start to want what they have. I want it *instead* of them rather than along *with* them. It prevents me from rejoicing at the success of those around me. It can make me angry and bitter, or withdrawn.

When someone excels at anything, rejoicing with them will be the most fulfilling. It should be a moment that inspires and motivates me to reach my potential. It should encourage me by knowing that it can be done. It is not impossible.

Envy will suffocate me. Joy will fulfill me.

Lord, draw the best out of me. Give me a generous heart that loves seeing others utilizing their gifts to the fullest. Let the success of others inspire me to greatness.

> "But when his brothers saw that their father loved him more
> than all his brothers, they hated him, and could not speak
> peaceably to him. Now Joseph had a dream, and when he told it
> to his brothers they only hated him the more." Genesis 37:4-5

> "And he said, 'What comes out of a man is what defiles a man.
> For from within, out of the heart of man, come evil thoughts,
> fornication, theft, murder, adultery, coveting, wickedness, deceit,
> licentiousness, envy, slander, pride, foolishness. All these evil
> things come from within, and they defile a man.'" Mark 7:20-23

What are the things that cause the most envy in my heart? What is the good I can focus on in that situation? How can I begin to rejoice in those moments instead?

TWENTY-TWO
About Me

So much is done for me; so much is given to me – I feel like I have a right to it all.

That attitude takes over during certain moments in my life. I develop a sense of entitlement that breeds a lack of gratitude and impartiality. I begin to think having things handed to me is normal and having what I want is fair.

Entitlement is dangerous. It can blind me to the needs around me. Getting what I deserve gets lost into getting what I *think* I deserve. It becomes about me, rather than about us, the community.

Lord, give me proper perspective. Help me to put my wants and desires second to my team, family and neighbor.

"What causes wars, and what causes fightings among you?
Is it not your passions that are at war in your members?
You desire and do not have; so you kill. And you covet and
cannot obtain; so you fight and wage war..." James 4:1-2

"For even when we were with you, we gave you this command:
If anyone will not work, let him not eat. For we hear that
some of you are walking in idleness, mere busybodies,
not doing any work. Now such persons we command and
exhort in the Lord Jesus Christ to do their work in quietness
and to earn their own living." 2 Thessalonians 3:10-12

Where do I see the spirit of entitlement creep into my life? How do I typically act when I have the spirit of entitlement? What are things I need to do to counter this?

Always be Grateful

I know that all I have has been given to me. My family, my talents, my faith, and my athletic ability are all gifts. What amazing gifts. Gratitude for these will keep me humble. Without this gratitude, I forget who I am and where I came from. It reminds me that I have needs I cannot meet by myself. It gives me the perspective I need to thrive. Otherwise I become confused, and that confusion causes my relationship with God to suffer. It causes my relationship with everyone to suffer.

Why do I forget these things? Gratitude needs to be as much a part of my life as the air I breathe. I am so grateful for all the little things in my life. I am grateful for the chance to be an athlete at this level. I am grateful for this moment.

Thank you Jesus, for everything. Thank you for your goodness and mercy. Thank you for making me and caring for me. Let me never forget this.

> "And whatever you do, in word or deed, do everything
> in the name of the Lord Jesus, giving thanks to God
> the Father through him." Colossians 3:17

> "Bless the Lord, O my soul, and forget not all his
> benefits, who forgives all your iniquity, who heals all
> your diseases, who redeems your life from the Pit, who
> crowns you with steadfast love and mercy, who satisfies
> you with good as long as you live..." Psalm 103:2-5

What are some things in my life I take for granted? How can I remember that those are gifts from the Lord? Where do I need to foster a spirit of gratitude in my life?

Showing Respect

I am driven. I like to succeed. These are things I am grateful for. They at times can also create a self-centered outlook. When I see opponents, I see an enemy. I become extremely critical of them and only care about their loss and my victory. This attitude makes it hard to show respect to others. I become so focused on me, that I fail to see them as a person striving for excellence as I am. I miss opportunities to show them respect when they excel. I miss a chance to honor them for good they do.

I do this off the field as well. I miss chances to love, or to see the good another is demonstrating, because I am distracted by my own desires. I blind myself.

Lord Jesus, help me to see the good that others do. Help me to respect those worthy of respect, to put my desires in proper perspective.

"love one another with brotherly affection; outdo
one another in showing honor." Romans 12:10

"So whatever you wish that men would do to you, do so to
them; for this is the law and the prophets." Matthew 7:12

When am I most likely to miss moments when people are excelling in front of me? Why do I miss those moments? How can I show people respect before/during/after competition? How can I honor people that demonstrate great integrity in their life?

To the End

Striving to do the right thing at every moment of every day can be exhausting. Sometimes I don't want to. Other times the temptation seems so strong I can't withstand it.

As an athlete and a Christian, there is a lot asked of me. Persevering through it all can seem daunting and outrageous. My humanity is broken, and I fail. There are times when I might justify it; there are times when I might put up a fight and lose. The important thing to realize is only by the grace given to me from God will the ability to persevere develop. By his grace and my cooperation with it, I can finish the race. I can be faithful.

Lord, your agony in the garden and on the cross must have tempted you to quit, but you never considered it. Give me the grace to persevere in all my commitments that bring you glory according to your will. Amen.

"Blessed is the man who endures trial, for when he has
stood the test he will receive the crown of life which God
has promised to those who love him." James 1:12

"And let us not grow weary in well-doing, for in due season
we shall reap, if we do not lose heart." Galatians 6:9

What are the things that seem the most daunting? When are the moments that make it hard to withstand temptation – when I am hungry, tired, bored, frustrated, etc.?

Jealousy

It can be easy to let jealousy grab a hold of my thoughts and words. Not wanting to lose my spot on the depth chart, my recognition among the fans and community, or my record, I begin to think only of myself. I am slowly reminded of what a lonely place that becomes. Jealousy does not elevate me to excel as a person. It doesn't even help as an athlete beyond perhaps a shallow moment of intense motivation.

To be jealous of what I have is to forget where it comes from in the first place. I have worked hard for things and my accomplishments, but in the end, they all come from God. If I can remember this, jealousy will have a smaller part in my life.

Sweet Jesus, thank you for my gifts and experiences. Inspire me in my moments of jealousy to let go of those things. Remind me that the effort is for you, not me. Detach me from things of this life so that I can more readily accept your grace.

> "For where jealousy and selfish ambition exist, there
> will be disorder and every vile practice." James 3:16

> "Love is patient and kind; love is not jealous or boastful;
> it is not arrogant or rude. Love does not insist on its own
> way; it is not irritable or resentful; it does not rejoice at
> wrong, but rejoices in the right." 1 Corinthians 13:4-6

What are the top three things I am attached to and get the most jealous over? What is the root of my jealousy – lust, pride, vanity, greed, etc? Are there moments that seem to bring jealousy out more than others? If so, what are they?

No Need

Athletes are high achievers. We get stuff done. This makes it understandable that many of us can have an air of self-reliance. We are invincible, in need of nothing. I can be like this. I think I am self-sufficient – that I have achieved so much, and thus can achieve even my own happiness.

I do this with my relationship with God. I think so highly of myself and what I can do, I tend to have a spiritual amnesia. I get into a groove and forget I can't do anything good apart from his grace. He drops on my priority list, at least until something happens to remind me how much I need him.

He is the reason for my achievements. If I develop a daily reminder of my need for God, I can effectively fight this.

Father, thank you for your patience with me. Give me the grace to always be child-like, depending entirely on you with great trust. Remind me each day to confess my complete need for you.

"since all have sinned and fall short of the
glory of God" Romans 3:23

"For by grace you have been saved through faith; and this is
not your own doing, it is the gift of God" Ephesians 2:8

"But when Jesus saw it he was indignant, and said to them,
'Let the children come to me, do not hinder them; for to such
belongs the kingdom of God. Truly, I say to you, whoever
does not receive the kingdom of God like a child shall
not enter it.' And he took them into his arms and blessed
them, laying his hands upon them." Mark 10:14-16

How does self-reliance manifest itself in my life? When are these moments destructive of my faith? How can I remind myself of my need for God on a daily basis? What does it mean to be child-like?

TWENTY-EIGHT

A Sacrificial Life

Sacrifice – I am used to this. I sacrifice my time and energy non-stop as an athlete. It is part of who I am. I leave blood, sweat, and, sometimes, tears on the field. But I am not the only one who has woven sacrifice throughout every fabric of their life.

It is impressive to think of the countless men and women over the last two thousand years who have sacrificed for God. Thousands and thousands have given everything for Jesus – their own life. That is sacrifice.

The martyrs (as they are called) give me a tremendous motivation. I am willing to do so much for my sport, but should pick up my game when it comes to my relationship with God. I need to follow the example of the martyrs. I need the same drive to sacrifice in my friendship with my Lord as I do in my sport.

Lord, you are my example of sacrifice. You laid it all on the line for me. Help me to have that same willingness to lay it all on the line for you.

"But he was wounded for our transgressions, he was bruised
for our iniquities; upon him was the chastisement that made
us whole, and with his stripes we are healed." Isaiah 53:5

"And they went to a place which was called Gethsemane; and
he said to his disciples, 'Sit here, while I pray.' And he took
with him Peter and James and John, and began to be greatly
distressed and troubled. And he said to them, 'My soul is very
sorrowful, even to death; remain here, and watch.' And going
a little farther, he fell on the ground and prayed that, if it were
possible, the hour might pass from him. And he said, 'Abba,
Father, all things are possible to thee; remove this cup from
me; yet not what I will, but what thou wilt.' And he came and
found them sleeping, and he said to Peter, 'Simon, are you
asleep? Could you not watch one hour?'" Mark 14:32-37

Where am I slacking in my relationship with the Lord? Why do I put more effort in my sport than my faith?

TWENTY-NINE

Desires

I think about what I want a lot.

I seem to do what I want a lot.

I sometimes let my desires take control. It is remarkable how powerful they can be.

A strong desire can distort a process, even if the goal is a good one. That process can take a wicked shape of its own – cheating, slandering, stealing, etc. If I want something bad enough, and it is something good, I need to work towards it the correct way. A desire for good things can lead people astray. I want to do it right. I want my desires to serve me, not control me.

Lord strengthen me. Heal me. Help me see clearly which way my desires are leading me: the right way or the wrong way.

"If then you have been raised with Christ, seek the
things that are above, where Christ is, seated at the right
hand of God. Set your minds on things that are above,
not on things that are on earth." Colossians 3:1-2

"But I say to you that everyone who looks at a woman lustfully has
already committed adultery with her in his heart." Matthew 5:28

Which desires seem to make the most noise in my life? What can I practically do to keep them in check? When has my desire for something good led me to seek it in the wrong fashion?

Good Fellowship

My whole career I have been used by others to win. Because of that, sometimes I feel alone. That makes it hard to trust people and feel deep connections. Do these people really care about me? Are they just fans? Isolating myself isn't the answer, but it's hard being around people that you can't completely trust.

I know I need to surround myself with good people. I can't make it alone. I need people guiding me in my walk with the Lord – and people to walk next to me. Friendships with other folks who are pursuing the Lord will be invaluable. They will help hold me accountable to what our Lord asks of me. They will help inspire me by their friendship and witness, and they will encourage me when I fall.

I need to find people that will challenge me to increase my love for Jesus and follow him more faithfully.

Lord, it is not good that man should be alone. Give me relationships that bring you glory!

"And Peter said to them, 'Repent, and be baptized every one of you in the name of Jesus Christ for the forgiveness of your sins; and you shall receive the gift of the Holy Spirit. For the promise is to you and to your children and to all that are far off, every one whom the Lord our God calls to him.' And he testified with many other words and exhorted them, saying, 'Save yourselves from this crooked generation.' So those who received his word were baptized, and there were added that day about three thousand souls. And they devoted themselves to the apostles' teaching and fellowship, to the breaking of bread and the prayers." Acts 2:38-42

"Two are better than one, because they have a good reward for their toil. For if they fall, one will lift up his fellow; but woe to him who is alone when he falls and has not another to lift him up." Ecclesiastes 4:9-10

Who are the people that pull me down? Who are the people that encourage me in my walk with the Lord? What changes do I need to make in my social life so that I am not putting my relationship with the Lord at risk?

Commitments

It can be hard to maintain a faithfulness to what I have committed. So many unforeseen demands on my time creep into my life. These are difficult to manage. Or it might be that a more appealing use of my time surfaces later that takes me off course.

As an athlete, I know the significance of staying faithful to training, to my team, and to my coach. For some reason, in life I lose that clarity and dedication. I need to stay faithful both to the little and big things in my life. When I say yes to something, I should follow through. When I am asked to do something, I shouldn't be flaky with my answer, holding out for something better to come along. I need to commit.

Father, make me a person of my word, being dedicated to what I know is good. Increase my faithfulness.

"He who is faithful in a very little is faithful also in much; and he is dishonest in a very little is dishonest also in much." Luke 16:10

"But above all, my brethren, do not swear, either by heaven or by earth or with any other oath, but let your yes be yes and your no be no, that you may not fall under condemnation." James 5:12

When is it hardest for me to stay faithful to commitments and promises I have made? Why is this hard for me? In what ways can it be damaging to go back on my commitments? Where am I afraid to actually make a commitment sometimes? What am I afraid of?

— THIRTY-TWO —

Visualize

Mental imagery is a valuable piece of preparation for my competition. It helps my confidence, my recovery, my ability to refocus, and, combined with my physical practice, improves my probability of success.

I should use this in my life as a disciple of Jesus Christ – which is even more important. For example, I can picture typical moments of temptation and the proper way to respond. Or, I can imagine a circumstance that might allow me to serve, or love, or forgive and help prepare my mind to help me make the right decision with God's grace. This imagery practice will help me recognize these moments as they occur in my life and not miss them. Hopefully I will be more attentive to the whispers of the Holy Spirit daily.

Lord, give me proper vision. Help me see the way life should be lived at every moment. Keep me attentive to the Holy Spirit always.

> "I will meditate on thy precepts, and fix my
> eyes on thy ways." Psalm 119:15

> "I keep the LORD always before me; because he is at
> my right hand, I shall not be moved." Psalm 16:8

How can I incorporate my mental imagery practice from sports into my Christian life? What are the types of moments I usually miss as a disciple? When is a good time to weave small moments of imagery into my life – perhaps during an examination of my day before bed?

Pray Always

My life, in many ways, is a prayer. When I act and speak in the hope of glorifying the Lord, it is a prayer. On the field, there are countless moments that can become prayer. Each stride, swing, or pass can be a moment of prayer when done for the glory of God. My life can exist with a tremendous integration of my faith and my sport. Adding this component of prayer to workouts and competition will heighten my purpose – it will all be for him.

What a great opportunity I have been given to turn countless moments doing what I love into gestures seeking to glorify the one I love – Jesus.

Lord, may my life always be a prayer. May I be a light on a hill, shining brightly in your name.

> "Rejoice always, pray constantly, give thanks in all circumstances; for this is the will of God in Christ Jesus for you." 1 Thessalonians 5:16-18

> "So, whether you eat or drink, or whatever you do, do all to the glory of God." 1 Corinthians 10:31

What is my "go to" way to pray as an athlete during practice and competition? How can I deepen those moments of prayer?

Hatred

Hate suffocates all life. It is a thief of joy. Its perceived motivation is a distortion that bears bitter fruit. It is something to be rejected. It is never good for me.

Hating my opponent should not be a motivation. If I play that out on the field, it doesn't end well. I easily lose control. Penalties don't help my team. Hatred doesn't have a place in athletics or the Christian life, nor should I be fooled to think so.

Jesus, cast out all hatred from my heart. Heal the source of hate, so that only love remains.

"If anyone says, 'I love God,' and hates his brother, he is a liar; for he who does not love his brother whom he has seen, cannot love God whom he has not seen." 1 John 4:20

"He who hates, dissembles with his lips and harbors deceit in his heart; when he speaks graciously, believe him not, for there are seven abominations in his heart;" Proverbs 26:24-25

What seems to stir up hatred in my heart the most? How can I control that feeling and turn it into something good? Why do I think hating my opponent is a good thing?

Forgiveness

Forgiveness is hard. Times come up when my teammates and coaches make huge mistakes, and sometimes they cost us big. It is upsetting. I work my tail off, and they screw up.

How should I deal with that?

To start, I should remind myself that we all make mistakes. We need forgiveness in our life over and over, so it is important that we give forgiveness over and over. When I don't forgive, bitterness grows in my heart. Bitterness doesn't make me Christ-like; it makes me mean. How quickly that will take me from being the one needing to forgive to the one needing to be forgiven.

Lord, you cried out during your crucifixion, "Father, forgive them." Make me more like you.

> "Then Peter came up and said to him, 'Lord, how often shall my brother sin against me, and I forgive him? As many as seven times?' Jesus said to him, 'I do not say to you seven times, but seventy times seven." Matthew 18:21-22

> "Put on then, as God's chosen ones, holy and beloved, compassion, kindness, lowliness, meekness, and patience, forbearing one another and, if one has a complaint against another, forgiving each other; as the Lord has forgiven you, so you also must forgive." Colossians 3:12-13

> "And when they came to the place which is called The Skull, there they crucified him, and the criminals, one on the right and one on the left. And Jesus said, 'Father, forgive them; for they know not what they do.' And they cast lots to divide his garments." Luke 23:33-34

When do I hold grudges? Why am I slow to forgive? Who do I need to forgive today?

One Hundred Percent

I get tired.

I get burned out.

I get bored.

I get distracted with things more fun.

I know I need to give 100% to what I have committed to. What good will it do me to cut my effort short? I gain nothing of value. I only weaken my resolve and heighten a twisted desire for self-gratification. Giving all my effort allows me the ability to glorify God and show him, through the effort, how grateful I am for the opportunity and talents.

Lord, I understand there will always be difficult things in life. Grant me the grace to give 100%, especially when it seems like my cross is too much to bear.

> "Whatever your task, work heartily, as serving
> the Lord and not men." Colossians 3:23

What prevents me from giving 100% - distractions, boredom, laziness? What is one thing I can start doing to improve the effort I put forth?

THIRTY-SEVEN

Examination

So often in athletics, a self-awareness is valuable. I spend time watching film, analyzing techniques, and discussing plans. This awareness can help me focus my efforts.

In my relationship with the Lord, this awareness is even more valuable. Taking time each night to review my walk with Christ from the day keeps me focused on the good and bad in my faithfulness to him. It sheds light on what I bring, or fail to bring, to our relationship. It helps create gratitude for his grace in my "success", and shows me in my "failures" what to work on. Without this awareness, I risk being blind, keeping things in darkness, or living a lie.

Holy Spirit, show me what I have done well and what I have done poorly today. Increase my self-awareness as it relates to my relationship with you.

> "If we say we have fellowship with him while we walk
> in darkness, we lie and do not live according to the
> truth; but if we walk in the light, as he is in the light,
> we have fellowship with one another, and the blood of
> Jesus his Son cleanses us from all sin." 1 John 1:6-7

> "He who conceals his transgressions will not prosper, but he who
> confesses and forsakes them will obtain mercy." Proverbs 28:13

Am I ever blind to my own faults? Do I notice the good that I do during the course of a day? Where can I find an *examination of conscience* to use each night? How can I be assured that this will help me without making me overly critical of myself?

Independence Gone Wrong

The ability to walk, talk, think, choose, compete, etc. are all given to me. As critical of myself that I can be at times, all the amazing things I have are gifts.

The world around me is filled with an air of self-sufficiency, of "I did it all myself." I am all for hard work and seeking opportunities, but when I take God out of the picture, I idolize myself. That never ends well. Everyone dies eventually. I am not my own little god. It is all given from the God of mercy.

I depend on you Lord, which at times seems completely counter to my life as an athlete. With my sport, I need to be free of most dependency, free of most weakness. With you it is all different. You are the reason I exist and you hold me into being. Independence from you is rebellion. I am actually grateful that I don't have to wade through life alone. There is such peace knowing of your providential care.

Jesus, let my heart sing praise to you always. Grow gratitude in my heart for you and all the gifts in my life.

> "Make a joyful noise to God, all the earth; sing the glory of his name; give to him glorious praise! Say to God, 'How terrible are thy deeds! So great is thy power that thy enemies cringe before thee. All the earth worships thee; they sing praises to thee, sing praises to thy name.'" Psalm 66:1-4

> "O give thanks to the Lord, call on his name, make known his deeds among the peoples!" 1Chronicles 16:8

When do I typically forget my dependency on the Lord? Why do I think I am self-sufficient, without need of God in the center of my life?

THIRTY-NINE

A Competitor

It is easy for me to get angry. I am a competitor. It is part of the territory. I like to succeed at what I do. Achieving less than I expect is upsetting. I have standards and goals. What is wrong with getting angry at myself if I don't hit them?

Nothing.

It all depends on where the anger leads me. It is important to acknowledge it and why I feel it, make a resolution or adjustment and then let it go. It is when I "keep" the anger inside that I put myself at risk.

Lord, give me the grace to acknowledge my anger and to keep it under control. Make me a person of meekness.

> "He who is slow to anger has great understanding, but he who has a hasty temper exalts folly. A tranquil mind gives life to the flesh, but passion makes the bones rot." Proverbs 14:29-30

> "But now put them all away: anger, wrath, malice, slander, and foul talk from your mouth." Colossians 3:8

What angers me? Why does it anger me? What adjustments do I need to keep it from building up? When does anger usually come back to bite me?

FORTY

Injury

So much of my life is wrapped up in my sport (some is great; some is not so great). That fact alone makes dealing with an injury difficult. When I am out, I feel disconnected, isolated, with a lot of unknown to deal with. Will I make it back as strong? Will I drop on the depth chart? With that, it's hard to just watch my team. There exists a bit of a distance between us, even if it is just in my head. I don't understand what God is doing in my life during these times.

Our Lord exhorted us to take up our cross daily (cf. Luke 9:23). These harsh moments in my life are not without purpose if I can open my eyes to see what the Lord desires of me in the experience. Things do not happen by chance. God has a plan for me through it all. Trust him. I am loved.

Lord help me to trust your plans in my life. Give me the grace to look for the good you will bring from each moment and each struggle.

"And after you have suffered a little while, the God of all
grace, who has called you to his eternal glory in Christ, will
himself restore, establish, and strengthen you." 1 Peter 5:10

"Count it all joy, my brethren, when you meet various trials, for
you know that the testing of your faith produces steadfastness.
And let steadfastness have its full effect, that you may be
perfect and complete, lacking in nothing." James 1:2-4

Do I trust that God has an amazing plan for my life? Why does injury send that trust down the drain? How can I trust that his plan is good even if I can't see it?

Heroic

The game winning shot, the clutch turnover, or the walk-off homer – who doesn't want to be the hero. I will take that any day and all day.

It's a wonderful thing to aspire for, but not everyone can be a hero in that sense…at least not all the time. Those are rare moments, sometimes reserved for the extremely talented freaks of nature.

Doing ordinary things in an extraordinary fashion can also be heroic, and I can do it all the time. If I help a teammate watching film, and do it with a selfless love, it can be heroic. If I open that door, or help someone up with immense love in my heart, I am being heroic. If love is my standard, my life will be heroic, because it will be worthy of imitation. It will become extraordinary. Besides, at the end of my life, Jesus won't ask me what freakish play I made; he will ask me how I loved.

Father, you showed your love for us by giving us Jesus. Increase love in my heart, especially in the quiet, hidden moments of my life.

"Let all that you do be done in love." 1 Corinthians 16:14

"By this we know love, that he laid down his life for us;
and we ought to lay down our lives for the brethren. But
if anyone has the world's goods and sees his brother in
need, yet closes his heart against him, how does God's
love abide in him? Little children, let us not love in word
or speech but in deed and in truth." 1 John 3:16-18

What are the moments that appear often in my life where I can bring great love? How can I remember to do these simple things with this love? Why is this sometimes difficult for me?

The Process

One rep at a time. One practice at a time. One competition at a time. You can't be great in a day. It takes time to build. I want to become something great. Knowing where I am going and how to get there set the path and process. Now I need patience to build it.

Jesus wants to be my foundation. I need to build our friendship patiently and wisely: one "yes" at a time, one moment at time, and one cross at a time. When I seek him one step at a time, I remain faithful to him. I know what the goal is – a deep friendship with him. I must allow him to do his part, and not be surprised at the ebbs and flows that will come as he purifies my love for him. As I patiently pursue this process, I let him work miracles in my life.

Lord, help me to put one foot in front of the other each day. Help me adhere to the process and patiently build.

> "For which of you, desiring to build a tower, does
> not first sit down and count the cost, whether he
> has enough to complete it?" Luke 14:28

> "Commit your way to the LORD; trust in
> him, and he will act." Psalm 37:5

What is the one step I need to achieve at this moment in my faith? What is one thing I can do today to build a stronger relationship with Jesus? When do I doubt he is present in this process and lose patience?

Staying Positive

Things will happen in my life that are out of my control – comments directed my way, accidents, sickness, etc. It is inevitable. These times can be heavy. They can weigh on my mind and heart for a while. The impact can be broad and perhaps deep.

What is within control is my attitude. If I maintain a positive attitude, I can limit the impact difficult moments will have on me. Struggles on the field, in the classroom, at work, and at home can wear down a good outlook. My attitude can keep me stable if I am able to direct it. A positive attitude really can make a tough moment bearable.

Lord, keep my eyes on you when I face difficult moments in my life. Don't let me develop a negative attitude that will suck joy out of my days.

> "A cheerful heart is a good medicine, but a downcast spirit dries up the bones." Proverbs 17:22

> "And above all these put on love, which binds everything together in perfect harmony. And let the peace of Christ rule in your hearts, to which indeed you were called in the one body. And be thankful." Colossians 3:14-15

When is my attitude typically the worst? What are the big things that wear down my positive attitude? How can I build up my attitude so it remains optimistic?

FORTY-FOUR
Unbreakable

Life can be hard. Athletics can be hard. Following Jesus can be hard. It isn't about *if* I get knocked down, it is about *when*. In that moment, how will I respond? Can I bounce back up and keep moving full-speed ahead? Or will I let this deflate me?

Being indomitable is to never be defeated, to never quit. At times, I let struggles shake my confidence or rattle my trust. If I begin to learn from these moments and not be surprised by them, I think I can handle them more effectively. That will help me respond with an unbreakable spirit.

Lord, help me to stand with my life on a solid foundation. Help me to trust in you and to never be afraid of a struggle. Help me to embrace my cross courageously and to always get up when I fall.

"Even though I walk through the valley of the shadow
of death, I fear no evil; for thou art with me; thy rod
and thy staff, they comfort me." Psalm 23:4

"For I am sure that neither death, nor life, nor angels,
nor principalities, nor things present, nor things to come,
nor powers, nor height, nor depth, nor anything else in
all creation, will be able to separate us from the love of
God in Christ Jesus our Lord." Romans 8:38-39

In my life, when is it hard to get back up? In what ways do I let getting knocked down deflate me? In my struggles, how can I maintain a confidence in the love that God has for me?

Priorities

I want to achieve so many things in my life. I also want to help as many people as possible. I understand, some days, so clearly what I have been given, and therefore what I must give in return. Yet, in my humanity, I am limited in what I can do. With good intentions, if I try to do too much, I will flutter around like a moth and get little done of significance.

I think the key is to prioritize what I would like to do, what I should do, and then what I can reasonably do well. Through prayer I can merge these three lists into one.

I know that my opportunity to leverage the influence I have as an athlete won't last forever. If I can prioritize the things the Lord might be asking of me, I will hopefully dive like an eagle with an extreme focus and intensity and leave a lasting impact.

Jesus, show me what my priorities should be. Give me a clear path and direction so I can serve you well.

"Do not lay up for yourselves treasures on earth, where moth and rust consume and where thieves break in and steal, but lay up for yourselves treasures in heaven, where neither moth nor rust consumes and where thieves do not break in and steal. For where your treasure is, there will your heart be also." Matthew 6:19-21

"But seek first his kingdom and his righteousness, and all these things shall be yours as well." Matthew 6:33

When will I pray through my priorities? How will I assure myself that I live by them?

A Role Model

I am a stellar athlete at a high level. When I make a big play, or set a record, people are inspired. That isn't enough. As a Christian athlete, I have a responsibility to use every bit of platform I stand on to point people, to lead people, to Jesus Christ.

It isn't enough to wow them with my skills and talents. I want to show them a life worth living. I hope to show a life lived in imitation of Jesus Christ. This desire must direct every area of my life. Only then will I be a role model.

Lord, give me the grace and ability to say the words of St. Paul – imitate me as I imitate Christ (see 1 Cor 11:1).

> "but whoever causes one of these little ones who
> believe in me to sin, it would be better for him to have
> a great millstone fastened round his neck and to be
> drowned in the depth of the sea." Matthew 18:6

> "Remember your leaders, those who spoke to you
> the word of God; consider the outcome of their
> life, and imitate their faith." Hebrews 13:7

Why do I glory in my fame rather than use it for God's glory? How can I live better as a role model, imitating Jesus? In what ways might I be leading people away from Jesus?

Not Quitting

It is tough to try my best all the time. It is tough to compete full throttle when I am not succeeding or have had a number of failures. It is easy to quit. I know there are times when quitting can be the right thing to do. But, too often, I want to quit because the other option is just simply *hard*. I don't think that is a good reason to quit. It doesn't help me develop character in difficult moments. It doesn't shape me into something better.

Quitting is too often driven by selfish, rather than prudent, reasons. If I live for me, things are going to just get more difficult. Nothing in this life is perfect. If I expect things to line up perfectly, as I see perfect, or quit, I will be doing a lot of quitting.

My Lord, you fell three times while carrying your cross and got up each time. Give me that same grit so that I don't quit simply because something is hard.

> "And let us not grow weary in well-doing, for in due season
> we shall reap, if we do not lose heart." Galatians 6:9

> "We are afflicted in every way, but not crushed; perplexed,
> but not driven to despair; persecuted, but not forsaken; struck
> down, but not destroyed; always carrying in the body the
> death of Jesus, so that the life of Jesus may also be manifested
> in our bodies. For while we live we are always being given
> up to death for Jesus' sake, so that the life of Jesus may be
> manifested in our mortal flesh." 2 Corinthians 4:8-11

Why does quitting become an option for me? What is the root of my temptation to quit? Who can I talk to when I feel like quitting to get a Christ-like perspective?

FORTY-EIGHT

Body and Soul

I was made in the image and likeness of God. Kind of wild to think about. Because he decided to make me in his image, I am able to think and choose. Life would be weird if I couldn't do those things. I wouldn't be human.

God clearly chose to give them to me for a purpose, to know him and love him. How I think and choose also matters to my body. There is an important connection between knowing, loving and doing that flows from being made in his image. The care I give to my body is helpful to my soul, and vice versa. Conversely, when I abuse my soul or body, it impacts the other in real ways.

I think too often in our world we forget this. For example, there is so much physical abuse to our bodies – sexual abuse, substance abuse, etc. This abuse impacts us spiritually. I think this is part of why so many people are lonely, sad, depressed and on the verge of despair.

If I live my life understanding the seriousness of the body-soul connection, hopefully I will experience the joys of God's original design – made in his image. With that, my life will put me on the path to experience the resurrection of my body and life everlasting in heaven.

Father, thank you for the gift of my mind and my heart. May I live in your image, utilizing the gifts you have given me for your sake.

"Do you not know that your body is a temple of the
Holy Spirit within you, which you have from God? You
are not your own; you were bought with a price. So
glorify God in your body." 1 Corinthians 6:19-20

"Have nothing to do with godless and silly myths. Train yourself
in godliness; for while bodily training is of some value, godliness
is of value in every way, as it holds promise for the present life
and also for the life to come. The saying is sure and worthy
of full acceptance. For to this end we toil and strive, because
we have our hope set on the living God, who is the Savior of
all men, especially of those who believe." 1 Timothy 4:7-10

What do I do with my body that will hurt my soul? What do I feed my soul (think all things media) that will hurt or exaggerate my natural desires too much? How can I change my actions?

The Dignity in Others

A key to success is knowing how to interact with people. In athletics, it is an integral aspect also. As a teammate, coach, or player, getting along with those around me is a priority. As a disciple of Jesus Christ, extending that to my neighbors and community is equally important.

One facet of getting along well with others is treating them with respect. To see them as likewise valued in our Lord's eyes with equal and innate dignity sets the groundwork for treating them well. From a friendly hello, to withholding a subjective judgment, respect will help me love like Jesus. It will help me build strong relationships. This will be especially imperative in my dating relationships. Our highly sexualized culture makes it easy to objectify someone rather than view them with profound dignity as God's child.

Lord, you respect my freedom. Teach me to respect others and treat them with profound dignity and love. Help me to honor the good I see in them.

"But we beseech you, brethren, to respect those who labor among you and are over you in the Lord and admonish you, and to esteem them very highly in love because of their work. Be at peace among yourselves." 1 Thessalonians 5:12-13

"Remind them to be submissive to rulers and authorities, to be obedient, to be ready for any honest work, to speak evil of no one, to avoid quarreling, to be gentle, and to show perfect courtesy toward all men. For we ourselves were once foolish, disobedient, led astray slaves to various passions and pleasures, passing our days in malice and envy, hated by men and hating one another;" Titus 3:1-3

Is there someone I consistently fail to show respect? What is something tangible I can do to honor and respect them, when appropriate? How can I improve bringing this respect into my dating relationships?

Legacy in Heaven

In my athletic facilities, there are banners and trophy cases all over the place. Awards are passed out every year. Will my name be on the wall? *Is* my name on the wall? Will I leave a legacy?

Is this the legacy I am hoping to leave?

Not everyone will have their name hanging from the rafters. Those that do have a tremendous opportunity to increase their impact. Those that don't have their name in the rafters can still leave a legacy, one perhaps far greater.

As a disciple of Jesus Christ, serving him faithfully and impacting the lives of those around me is the best type of legacy. Helping to change a life, and all those impacted by that changed life, is like getting a banner in the rafters of heaven. The reward will be abundant there, for the angels will see and rejoice.

Lord, make me an instrument of the gospel. May I be a light on the hill. Help my legacy leave an impact on eternity.

> "For, 'every one who calls upon the name of the Lord will
> be saved.' But how are men to call upon him in whom
> they have not believed? And how are they to believe in
> him of whom they have never heard? And how are they to
> hear without a preacher? And how can men preach unless
> they are sent? As it is written, 'How beautiful are the feet
> of those who preach good news!'" Romans 10:13-15

> "For I am already on the point of being sacrificed; the time of my
> departure has come. I have fought the good fight, I have finished
> the race, I have kept the faith. Henceforth there is laid up for
> me the crown of righteousness, which the Lord, the righteous
> judge, will award to me on that Day, and not only to me but
> also to all who have loved his appearing." 2 Timothy 4:6-8

What legacy do I want to leave? How do I need to adjust my life in order to achieve that legacy? What help do I need to make these adjustments?

FIFTY-ONE

Planting my Flag

It was a common practice to "plant your flag" when you captured a territory in war, or claimed property as your own. Your flag marked your turf, and you defended it if the need arose. In athletics, it is analogous to your end zone, or your end of the court. You stand your ground and defend it.

With the Lord, there is a similar "flag planting" that should take place in my life: to stand with the Lord and lay claim to being his disciple. The tough part is to never move away from the Lord and to defend that position no matter what comes my way – temptation, ridicule, suffering, doubt, etc.

I pray for the courage and grace to plant my flag, to stand my ground, and to never be moved.

Lord, you are my King and my God. Lend me the tenacity to never leave your side and drift away.

> "Therefore, my beloved brethren, be steadfast, immovable, always abounding in the work of the Lord, knowing that in the Lord your labor is not in vain." 1 Corinthians 15:58

> "For freedom Christ has set us free; stand fast therefore, and do not submit again to a yoke of slavery." Galatians 5:1

When am I most tempted to drift away from the Lord? Why are these moments tempting? What would help me stand my ground with him more faithfully?

Proper Expectations

Society today honors and awards success, not failure. The job market, the stock market, and the academic world all promote success. This can make failure a hard pill to swallow. I don't get awarded for failing.

Do I let mistakes weigh heavily on me? If I do, maybe it means I have the wrong expectations. I will never be free from failure. I shouldn't expect that.

Instead, maybe I should focus on never *wanting* to fail yet realizing at times I will. This outlook should help me be motivated by my mistakes rather than defeated by them. This can make a vast difference in the way I approach my game, my responsibilities, or my relationship with the Lord.

Never desire to fail, yet never be surprised when I do. Seek the support I need, and create the proper expectations for myself. I like this plan.

Lord, thank you for this insight. Help every mistake I make increase my desire to improve.

> "but he said to me, 'My grace is sufficient for you, for
> my power is made perfect in weakness.' I will all the
> more gladly boast of my weaknesses, that the power of
> Christ may rest upon me." 2 Corinthians 12:9-10

> "He drew me up from the desolate pit, out of the miry bog, and
> set my feet upon a rock, making my steps secure. He put a new
> song in my mouth, a song of praise to our God. Many will see
> and fear, and put their trust in the LORD." Psalm 40:2-3

What is the biggest struggle with failure that I face? How can I improve my outlook on failure so that it encourages me rather than suppresses me?

Priceless

How can I really be priceless? I am just another player, used to win games like all the others that have gone before me. I am replaceable. The light that shines on me will fade; in fact, it can shut off at any moment. It is a man-made light, shining a man-made glory. I am not priceless.

This all changes when I look from God's perspective. In his eyes, I am priceless. My infinite worth comes from him as his creature made in his image and likeness. On top of that, his grace changed me when I professed faith in him and was baptized. I became his son; I became his daughter. No man-made anything can change that. Nothing can alter the great and passionate love he has for me. That is why I actually *am* priceless.

Father, at times I fail to understand how intense your love is for me. My brokenness sometimes limits my ability to comprehend your perfect, unfailing love. Teach me about the boundless love you have for me.

> "For God so loved the world that he gave his only
> Son, that whoever believes in him should not
> perish but have eternal life." John 3:16

> "No longer do I call you servants, for the servant does not know
> what his master is doing; but I have called you friends, for all
> that I have heard from my Father I have made known to you.
> You did not choose me, but I chose you and appointed you that
> you should go and bear fruit and that your fruit should abide; so
> that whatever you ask the Father in my name, he may give it to
> you. This I command you, to love one another." John 15:15-17

What do I tell myself that goes against the truth that I am priceless? Why? How can I more fully comprehend the worth that I do in fact have as God's creation?

Finding Peace

When I incorporate prayer in my life, I am at peace. Being at peace is a big deal. It helps me exist in the present moment. I know how significant it is to be fully in the moment. I am more likely to hit my potential – on the field, and in showing love to those around me off the field.

Prayer brings me peace, because it connects me to the source of my being. The God of love, the God of Mercy, Father, Son and Holy Spirit, communicates with me and speaks into my heart and soul. He desires to spend time with me. This daily conversation is changing my life in ways I can't imagine. How blessed I am to have center stage with the God of the universe in prayer.

Lord, forgive me when I fail to pray. Pour your grace down upon me, so that I may never refuse to spend time with you in prayer.

"Likewise the Spirit helps us in our weakness; for we do not
know how to pray as we ought, but the Spirit himself intercedes
for us with sighs too deep for words." Romans 8:26

"For God is not a God of confusion but
of peace..." 1 Corinthians 14:33

What keeps me from praying on a daily basis? How can I deepen my time of prayer? Who can help me learn to pray with Scripture?

On and Off the Field

When a competition isn't going my way, it can be disheartening. In my life, moments that don't go my way can also seem disheartening. I have a tremendous opportunity as an athlete to grow in character which can help me in these moments. I have been given a chance to participate in a fantastic training ground for life.

What I do in a game that isn't going my way can transfer perfectly to those similar moments in my life. Will I quit or will I persevere to the end? What I do on the field will likely carry over into my life. Quitting in life and faith is not an option, nor should it be on the field.

Lord God, put your hand upon me in these moments so that I may always seek your glory. Help me continue to the end, desiring to please you in those opportunities.

> "More than that, we rejoice in our sufferings, knowing that suffering produces endurance, and endurance produces character, and character produces hope, and hope does not disappoint us, because God's love has been poured into our hearts through the Holy Spirit who has been given to us." Romans 5:3-5

> "Count it all joy, my brethren, when you meet various trials, for you know that the testing of your faith produces steadfastness. And let steadfastness have its full effect, that you may be perfect and complete, lacking in nothing." James 1:2-4

What is my typical response when things don't seem to be going my way? How can I adjust my attitude so that I stay positive and persevere? In what ways can I assure myself the lessons I learn on the field will also apply in my life off the field?

Daily Sacrifice

To give until it hurts and to keep giving – that is the standard. I appreciate the challenge Jesus mentioned. He said we must carry our cross if we are to be His disciples. Why does this challenge seem so hard to some, when others seem to be motivated by it? How do I respond to this? Hopefully well.

I wasn't made for "easy". That will slowly suffocate my soul. I was made for sacrifice – it is when I give of myself that I will bear fruit. It is when I truly sacrifice that I will be fulfilled.

Lord, you are the greatest example of sacrifice. May I, by your grace, imitate you in this. Help me to die for love of you, as you died for love of me.

> "Truly, truly, I say to you, unless a grain of wheat
> falls into the earth and dies, it remains alone; but
> if it dies, it bears much fruit." John 12:24

> "Then Jesus told his disciples, 'If any man would
> come after me, let him deny himself and take up
> his cross and follow me.'" Matthew 16:24

When do I choose "easy"? When do I need to give more of myself for the sake of God and neighbor? How can I incorporate little sacrifices into my daily life?

Guiding my Desires

At times my desires are messed up. They drive me towards stuff that isn't good for me. As an athlete, I have a lot of temptations in front of me that feed my desires. With that, I have a great responsibility to control them and direct them to a good.

I need to work with the Lord and let him purify my desires. With his grace building upon my disciplined life of training on the field, the potential to have control of my desires is huge. If I couple this with daily prayer, I will be allowing our Lord to work miracles in my life. As I pray, the Lord teaches me more about himself…and more about me. Both of these are necessary and will help me know when my desires are leading me the wrong way.

Lord, help me bring to light the dark desires in my heart that keep me from running closer to you.

> "For those who live according to the flesh set their minds on the things of the flesh, but those who live according to the Spirit set their minds on the things of the Spirit." Romans 8:5

> "What causes wars, and what causes fightings among you? Is it not your passions that are at war in your members? You desire and do not have; so you kill. And you covet and cannot obtain; so you fight and wage war. You do not have, because you do not ask. You ask and do not receive, because you ask wrongly, to spend it on your passions." James 4:1-3

In what ways can I cooperate with God to purify my desires? Which desire do I want to focus on right now? What desires am I keeping in the dark?

Motivated by Hate

When I let hate be a frequent motivation on the field, I risk letting it motivate other areas of my life. It can seep into my relationships with my teammates – when they make a mistake, or if they start in front of me. I will more readily hate friends or classmates when they annoy me or "get in my way".

I am naïve if I think the dangers of hate don't exist in my life. I risk limiting my potential as an athlete if I let hate be an important source of motivation for me. I risk becoming dependent upon it.

Father, bring me peace when I feel hatred. Help me to see past the source of hatred and see your creation in all its goodness.

"He who conceals hatred has lying lips, and he
who utters slander is a fool." Proverbs 10:18

"But I say to you, Love your enemies and pray for
those who persecute you," Matthew 5:44

Do I let hate motivate me on the field? What can I do to change this? How has hatred manifested itself in my relationships? What can I do to decrease this?

With the Eyes of Christ

When I look at the world, do I see things as Christ sees them? Do I see grace in the midst of suffering? Do I see hope instead of despair?

The way I view reality is significant. Without the proper vision, I risk going the wrong direction. To follow Jesus and give him everything is where I must start. To invite others to this life is where I go next.

My friends, my time, my dating relationships, my hobbies, my music, my books, my TV, and my movies: do I look at these as Jesus does, as Jesus wants me to? If not, I should invite him into these areas of my life.

Dear Lord, help to see as you see. I invite you into all the areas of my life so that I may please you in them and see them with your eyes.

"The unspiritual man does not receive the gifts of the Spirit of God, for they are folly to him, and he is not able to understand them because they are spiritually discerned." 1 Corinthians 2:14

"Do not be conformed to this world but be transformed by the renewal of your mind, that you may prove what is the will of God, what is good and acceptable and perfect." Romans 12:2

What am I not seeing correctly? How can I begin to see as our Lord sees? How do my friends, time, dating relationships, hobbies, music, books, TV and movies impact my friendship with Jesus? Am I afraid to invite Jesus into these areas of my life, and if so why?

My Community

I play with a city, state, or name on my back. I represent a local community. I am a public figure to some degree. What a great blessing this is for me. I have an opportunity to contribute to the betterment of society. I can seek, with my peers, to build up the common good, to serve the people of this community.

This is a great calling – to live outside myself. The early Christians sought to be servants, especially to the outcasts and less fortunate. They, in a very real way, changed the world one act of love at a time. This is within my capacity – do one act of service at a time to make my community a better place.

Jesus, give me the heart of a servant. Give me the courage to do one act of love at a time.

> "Above all hold unfailing your love for one another, since love covers a multitude of sins. Practice hospitality ungrudgingly to one another. As each has received a gift, employ it for one another, as good stewards of God's varied grace:" 1 Peter 4:8-10

> "Jesus replied, 'A man was going down from Jerusalem to Jericho, and he fell among robbers, who stripped him and beat him, and departed, leaving him half dead. Now by chance a priest was going down that road; and when he saw him he passed by on the other side. So likewise a Levite, when he came to the place and saw him, passed by on the other side. But a Samaritan, as he journeyed, came to where he was; and when he saw him, he had compassion, and went to him and bound up his wounds, pouring on oil and wine; then he set him on his own beast and brought him to an inn, and took care of him. And the next day he took out two denarii and gave them to the innkeeper, saying, 'Take care of him; and whatever more you spend, I will repay you when I come back.'" Luke 10:30-35

In what way can I serve my team, my roommates, my campus, and my community? What excuses do I allow to get in the way? Where can I go to find opportunities to serve?

Inspiring Others

They say leaders draw potential out of people. I would love to help inspire my teammates, and others around me, to give 100% all the time. I would love to help them reach their potential. I know how powerful it can be to help someone recognize what they have inside them. We all need that.

The world would be a much better place if we built each other up rather than tore each other down. I mean that in the right way, not the fluffy "agree with everything so they feel good" way.

When I look at people, I need to recognize the slightest good in them and concentrate on that. If I do that, I can encourage and motivate them. That is always a noble thing.

Father, let me look upon those around me with affection, and inspire them to reach the potential you have given them.

> "Therefore encourage one another and build one another up, just as you are doing." 1 Thessalonians 5:11

> "Iron sharpens iron, and one man sharpens another." Proverbs 27:17

Who is one person I can encourage today to strive towards his potential? How can I make this a habit? What does it mean to be iron sharpening iron?

My Source

There are a lot of things going on in this world. My life could go a lot of different ways.

I want Jesus to set the tone for my life and direction. I want him to keep my decisions from being arbitrary or self-centered. I need him to do that. When this happens, the temptation to drift from my commitments will decrease, because he will be the reason for them. This will come with consistent conversation with him and listening to his voice in the mundane moments of my day. When I make that a habit, he will be my rock. He will be my motivation. He will be my source.

My Lord and my God, I believe, help my unbelief. May you forever be my foundation.

> "And without faith it is impossible to please him. For whoever would draw near to God must believe that he exists and that he rewards those who seek him." Hebrews 11:6

> "Everyone then who hears these words of mine and does them will be like a wise man who built his house upon the rock; and the rain fell, and the floods came, and the winds blew and beat upon that house, but it did not fall, because it had been founded on the rock." Matthew 7:24-25

When is my faith challenged the most? Can I pray, "Lord, increase my faith!" on a daily basis? What aspects of Jesus and his teachings do I have the hardest part with? How can I seek to understand those in greater depth?

SIXTY-THREE
Seeking Forgiveness

There are days when the last thing I want to do is concede I am wrong. I don't know if anyone likes to admit mistakes, but I do not. It gets harder the bigger the mistake. Ironically, that might be the most important time to seek forgiveness. If I want to contribute to the betterment of the team, or any of my relationships, I need to ask forgiveness when I am in the wrong.

It is great practice for me anyways. I daily mess up in my relationship with the Lord. Learning how to seek forgiveness is paramount for my relationship with him. Thankfully he is eager to forgive.

Lord, preserve a unity in my relationships by helping me readily seek forgiveness when need be. Keep me humble.

"Two men went into the temple to pray, one a Pharisee and the other a tax collector. The Pharisee stood and prayed thus with himself, 'God, I thank thee that I am not like other men, extortioners, unjust, adulterers, or even like this tax collector. I fast twice a week, I give tithes of all that I get.' But the tax collector, standing far off, would not even lift up his eyes to heaven, but beat his breast, saying, 'God, be merciful to me a sinner!' I tell you, this man went down to his house justified rather than the other; for every one who exalts himself will be humbled, but he who humbles himself will be exalted." Luke 18:10-14

"for a righteous man falls seven times, and rises again..." Proverbs 24:16

When am I least likely to seek needed forgiveness? What fears keep me from asking for it? Why is it hard for me to admit I am wrong?

A Good Player

I think back to all the coaches I have played for over the years. Yes, some have been much better than others, but I owe a lot to all of them. Even so, I can criticize a bad coach with ease. It is easy to get caught up in the "injustice" of not getting the playing time I want, or to overreact at the "harsh" assessment a coach might readily hand out.

I know, in the end, I can't really make a coach a better coach. What I can do is become a better player. I can be loyal, responsive, positive, and a role model to my teammates. I can walk the walk, not just play lip service. I can do what is asked of me to the best of my ability. When I do that, I become the right type of player for any type of coach.

Being a good player will also help me be a better disciple: loyal, responsive, positive, and a role model. The traits are so similar. It really is a win-win.

Thank you, Lord, for this gift of being an athlete. There are so many ways that being an athlete helps me as your disciple. May your grace help me improve.

> "Not every one who says to me, 'Lord, Lord,' shall
> enter the kingdom of heaven, but he who does the will
> of my Father who is in heaven." Matthew 7:21

> "Show yourself in all respects a model of good deeds, and
> in your teaching show integrity, gravity, and sound speech
> that cannot be censured, so that an opponent may be put
> to shame, having nothing evil to say of us." Titus 2:7-8

Why do I focus on my coach's issues rather than myself as a player? What top two areas can I focus on to become better in this regard? What are the negative similarities I possess as a player and a disciple? What about the positive ones?

Have Courage

The people I typically admire had the courage to be different. They forged through tough moments of doubt, criticism, failure, or at times immense loss. They stood up and challenged the popular thought, or defended someone, or something, in need of defense.

To become great, it is clear I need courage.

Being courageous isn't being rash, or nuts. It means I am willing to do something despite feeling fear. In fact, if I don't feel fear, I am actually not being courageous. Jesus had the courage to go to his Passion despite his agony in the garden. The Apostles eventually had the courage to go out and evangelize the world despite locking themselves in the upper room during the crucifixion of our Lord. I will often feel fear. It is in those moments that I need to act courageously.

Father, give me the courage I need to be faithful to what you have called me to do, for your glory, in your name.

> "fear not, for I am with you, be not dismayed, for I am your God; I will strengthen you, I will help you, I will uphold you with my victorious right hand." Isaiah 41:10

> "Now who is there to harm you if you are zealous for what is right? But even if you do suffer for righteousness' sake, you will be blessed. Have no fear of them, nor be troubled, but in your hearts reverence Christ as Lord. Always be prepared to make a defense to any one who calls you to account for the hope that is in you, yet do it with gentleness and reverence;" 1 Peter 3:13-15

What are the challenges I face on a regular basis that cause fear? How can I respond with courage?

Give the Gift

Jesus died and rose from the dead. He did that so I could be freed from sin and death and be with him in an intimate relationship now and for eternity in heaven. What a great gift. To follow him as his disciple is to seek to know him, love him and make him known to those who don't yet know him.

At some level, I have a platform as an athlete. It might be small (or it might be big), but nonetheless I have it. The Lord has given me this great gift to be on this team, to excel at this sport - to be one of a very small group of individuals here and now. What will I do with that gift? Will I respond to this call and responsibility to help others know the gift that is being offered to them? Will I give the gift I have been given?

Jesus, help me have the courage to talk about you like I do so many other things. Let me not be ashamed of the gospel.

"And Jesus came and said to them, 'All authority in heaven and on earth has been given to me. Go therefore and make disciples of all nations, baptizing them in the name of the Father and of the Son and of the Holy Spirit, teaching them to observe all that I have commanded you; and lo, I am with you always, to the close of the age.'" Matthew 28:18-20

"For, 'every one who calls upon the name of the Lord will be saved.' But how are men to call upon him in whom they have not believed? And how are they to believe in him of whom they have never heard? And how are they to hear without a preacher? And how can men preach unless they are sent? As it is written, 'How beautiful are the feet of those who preach good news!" Romans 10:13-15

How many opportunities to talk about Jesus do I miss? When am I most fearful to preach the gospel? Why? How can I prepare myself to more effectively talk about Jesus to others?

Defining Me

When I wear my gear, I feel stronger. My confidence is boosted. I am an athlete. Everyone can see it when I wear it. I love it. Some days I need to do it. It defines me.

But really, why do I need this? Am I so dependent upon this image? Why does it matter if people know me as an athlete or not? Am I not good enough as a person apart from my athletic ability? Am I this weak, or this insecure?

Who I am is more than the image I portray. My confidence should not lie in my abilities and talents. It should lie in the reality that I am loved beyond understanding. That is what brings a lasting confidence. That is what brings a lasting peace and joy. From there, I can live with strength. When I understand this, the image I portray will be a powerful image of a child of God who cannot be moved.

Jesus, give me confidence in my worth and goodness. Make me strong in this unending truth.

> "Whoever confesses that Jesus is the Son of God, God abides in him, and he in God. So we know and believe the love God has for us. God is love, and he who abides in love abides in God, and God abides in him. In this is love perfected with us, that we may have confidence for the day of judgment, because as he is so are we in this world. There is no fear in love, but perfect love casts out fear..." 1 John 4:15-18

What is the exact image I cling to? When is it the hardest to let go? Who am I trying to impress this image upon most in my life? What gets in the way from understanding I am a beloved child of God?

My Number One

God, family, sport. This is how I claim to live. This is how I see dozens of athletes and coaches claim to live.

What do I do in my life that makes this evident? Do I really make God #1, family #2, and everything else after that? Does that mean I am not caring enough about being an athlete?

Well, I think it means I've got my priorities straight. My athletic ability is such a blessing and has given me amazing opportunities. But, to make that my "god" is to live a lie. It all came from the Lord; he should remain at the top. My family, if I am blessed to have one, should be next. The Lord gave them to me and me to them. Loving them is my duty.

If I let my priorities get out of whack, everything will collapse. I will lose vision. I will live in confusion.

Jesus Christ, don't let me hide you in a closet. Stay at the center of my life.

> "Woe to you, scribes and Pharisees, hypocrites! for you tithe mint and dill and cummin, and have neglected the weightier matters of the law, justice and mercy and faith; these you ought to have done, without neglecting the others." Matthew 23:23

> "He who pursues righteousness and kindness will find life and honor." Proverbs 21:21

> "As for the saints in the land, they are the noble, in whom is all my delight. Those who choose another god multiply their sorrows; their libations of blood I will not pour out or take their names upon my lips." Psalm 16:3-4

When do I see myself drifting away from God as my number one priority? What is the biggest cause of this? What adjustments in this regard need to be made?

A Desire to Inspire

I want to be an inspiration. I want to do something heroic.

I want to do this in a way that doesn't make it all about me. Vanity can be a big player in this desire if I am not careful, and if it comes from a desire for others to recognize me. I am vain if I want others to toot my horn.

The desire to inspire can still be a great thing. If I can live my life in a way that reflects truth, goodness, and beauty, then I can be a necessary inspiration to those around me. I will be showing them aspects of God in a world that is in desperate need of him. That will be heroic, although perhaps without the stardom of the world. That is *okay*. The saints are perfect examples of this. Heroes who, usually, had no fame accompanying them but so wonderfully showed others the face of Christ. They are the ones that change the world in a positive way. They are inspiring.

My Lord, may I always be a reflection of you. Make me a hero in the same manner of the holy men and women who have gone before me.

> "Beware of practicing your piety before men in order to be
> seen by them; for then you will have no reward from your
> Father who is in heaven. Thus, when you give alms, sound no
> trumpet before you, as the hypocrites do in the synagogues
> and in the streets, that they may be praised by men. Truly,
> I say to you, they have received their reward. But when you
> give alms, do not let your left hand know what your right
> hand is doing, so that your alms may be in secret; and your
> Father who sees in secret will reward you." Matthew 6:1-4

How can my life reflect truth, beauty and goodness? In what ways does vanity take shape in my life? How can I act counter to my vanity?

My Speech

Speaking without thinking is not usually a good thing. I use my tongue in ways that get me in trouble. It is impossible to lasso the words coming out of my mouth in the hopes of shoving them back in. Once they leave, they are gone.

My words can cause tremendous harm, especially because people look up to me. My words also can cause *me* harm, harm to my soul: when I gossip, slander, yell harsh criticism or sarcasm, and tear down others. The list goes on and on.

My life is short. I need to use it to build up others rather than tear them down. If I don't recognize the power of my words, they will likely come back to bite me.

Lord, your words are everlasting life. Give me the grace to speak words of hope and encouragement.

> "He who keeps his mouth and his tongue keeps
> himself out of trouble." Proverbs 21:23

> "For every kind of beast and bird, of reptile and sea creature,
> can be tamed and has been tamed by humankind, but no
> human being can tame the tongue – a restless evil, full
> of deadly poison. With it we bless the Lord and Father,
> and with it we curse men, who are made in the likeness of
> God. From the same mouth come blessing and cursing.
> My brethren, this ought not to be so." James 3:7-10

When do I let my tongue run wild? How do I speak about the opposite sex, my teammates, or my coaches? Do I seek to build up others or tear them down more with my words? What is one simple resolution I can make to improve?

Losing Well

There is a way to do everything well – even losing. It doesn't mean liking it, or enjoying the process. It means I do it with grace and character.

To lose well is to recognize the good in my opponent: the effort, the talent, the preparation, etc. It means not making excuses and rightly acknowledging the loss. It means controlling my temper and finishing the competition as a noble competitor who has met his match.

The practice of not placing blame and recognizing a factual outcome will be a great blessing as a Christian. It prepares me to acknowledge my shortcomings and ask for the grace to overcome them. It helps me accept responsibility for my thoughts and actions as a follower of Jesus without blaming someone else or justifying them.

My Lord, all that you have created is good. Give me eyes to see this truth, especially when I am not victorious.

"Do not withhold good from those to whom it is due,
when it is in your power to do it." Proverbs 3:27

"One of the criminals who were hanged railed at him, saying,
'Are you not the Christ? Save yourself and us!' But the other
rebuked him, saying, 'Do you not fear God, since you are under
the same sentence of condemnation? And we indeed justly; for
we are receiving the due reward of our deeds; but this man has
done nothing wrong.' And he said, 'Jesus, remember me when
you come in your kingdom.' And he said to him, 'Truly, I say to
you, today you will be with me in Paradise.'" Luke 23:39-43

When is losing the most difficult for me? What is my typical reaction? What should I change so that I lose well? Which actions do I most easily justify that cause a separation between me and my Lord?

To Live for Others

It is easy to do things for myself. It is not hard at all to choose "number one". The urges I have, the desires I feel – those are easy to put at the top of the to-do list. My success often feeds this self-centered outlook. What I will discover at the end of this road is loneliness and insecurity.

Being a role model is to think of Jesus first, my neighbor second. If I were to become the greatest of all time in my sport, the legacy wouldn't be impactful…unless my life is lived in the service of God and neighbor. If I strive to imitate Christ, and try to be a saint, by God's grace I can inspire people to do the same. If that happens, the world will be a better place…and heaven might be fuller.

Lord, make me an instrument of inspiration. Give me the desire to show people the path that leads to you.

> "and like living stones be yourselves built into a spiritual house, to be a holy priesthood, to offer spiritual sacrifices acceptable to God through Jesus Christ." 1 Peter 2:5

> "And if you be unwilling to serve the Lord, choose this day whom you will serve, whether the gods your fathers served in the region beyond the River, or the gods of the Amorites in whose land you dwell; but as for me and my house, we will serve the Lord." Joshua 24:15

Why do I choose my needs first in so many instances? How will a self-centered life lead me to a lonely life? What inspires me the most about being a role model?

To the End

As an athlete, quitting usually isn't part of the gig. As a Christian, quitting shouldn't be either. It is hard to live the Christian life. It is hard to be faithful. Jesus said we will need to pick up our crosses and carry them.

As I think more about the countless men and women who have been tortured and killed because of their Christian faith, I have no reason to quit. The martyrs are tremendous witnesses of faith and perseverance. They were stretched to the limit. I flirt with quitting for far less severe reasons.

Jesus is Lord. He is the way, the truth and the life. Being his disciple, while not always easy, is the purpose of *my* life. Fulfillment comes when I invite him into the center of it. I need to trust him and his plan that I be with him in heaven. This life is hard because of sin. It will end. Heaven will be more than I can ever imagine.

Lord, I thank you for the men and women who have gone before me, who you have raised up as an example of living as your disciple to the very end. Now help me to imitate them as they imitated you.

> "Never flag in zeal, be aglow with the Spirit, serve the
> Lord. Rejoice in your hope, be patient in tribulation,
> be constant in prayer." Romans 12:11-12

> "Then they will deliver you up to tribulation, and put
> you to death; and you will be hated by all nations for my
> name's sake. And then many will fall away, and betray one
> another, and hate one another. And many false prophets
> will arise and lead many astray. And because wickedness
> is multiplied, most men's love will grow cold. But he who
> endures to the end will be saved." Matthew 24:9-13

Is my dedication to my sport greater than my dedication to God? If so, why? What makes it hard to follow Jesus to the end? Which martyr can I read about to help inspire me to never quit?

SEVENTY-FOUR

See the Good

When things don't happen as I hope they would, my positive attitude can be an invaluable asset. Sometimes, the idea of having a positive attitude can seem cheesy – like a greeting card. "See the glass half-full." There are days when that seems like a banner in a Kindergarten class.

In reality, it is extremely difficult to do. I have a genuine admiration for individuals that can see things in a positive light. I understand that doesn't mean we ignore the difficulty or live in a fantasy world. It means that we see reality as disciples of Christ. God allows all things for His glory. We know we are called to follow him in the good and bad times. The suffering is a great gift if we united it to Jesus on the cross. When this happens, we can find joy in our cross.

Lord, allow me to have such a great trust in you that I begin to see the positive aspects in my struggles. May my attitude always draw me closer to you and to a greater love of those around me.

"Now I rejoice in my sufferings for your sake, and in my flesh I complete what is lacking in Christ's afflictions for the sake of his body, that is, the church," Colossians 1:24

"Praise the LORD! Praise God in his sanctuary; praise him in his mighty firmament! Praise him for his mighty deeds; praise him according to his exceeding greatness! Praise him with trumpet sound; praise him with lute and harp! Praise him with timbrel and dance; praise him with strings and pipe! Praise him with sounding cymbals; praise him with loud clashing cymbals! Let everything that breathes praise the LORD! Praise the LORD!" Psalm 150

How can I practice having a positive attitude? What are some helpful triggers to remind myself to stay optimistic? How can I praise the Lord when I feel frustrated?

Fruit of My Anger

No one is perfect. Spending time with people can make that evident, very quickly. Their quirks, their nuances, and their defects can all take me to a place I don't like to go, a place of anger.

I know that feeling angry isn't bad in itself, unless I let it get the best of me. When it does, I do things I normally wouldn't. It has a canny ability to stir up in me hatred, rash reactions, bitterness, or the tendency to say/do something I'll regret. It is vital to be aware of myself and to recognize when a slight annoyance starts to turn into anger. As I begin to recognize that, I can begin to keep it under control.

Father, help me to look on others with mercy, as you look upon me. Heal the anger in my heart I feel towards others. Make me a source of love not rancorous criticism.

"A hot tempered man stirs up strife, but he who is
slow to anger quiets contention." Proverbs 15:18

"But I say to you that every one who is angry with his
brother shall be liable to judgment; whoever insults his
brother shall be liable to the council, and whoever says, 'You
fool!' shall be liable to the hell of fire." Matthew 5:22

How do I negatively react when I get angry? Why is this my reaction? How can I remember to focus on the good I see in someone rather than the negative?

Right Now

All I have is now. The past is done, and the future is not yet here. I have this moment, this chance.

The present moment provides me an opportunity to do the greatest of all things – to love. My challenge is to fight with everything I have to be fully engaged in the moment before me: to avoid distractions, to stop thinking of myself and my needs, and to think only of the person in front of me and his or her needs.

To love well, I need to be in the moment – in the here and now. So many moments have come and gone, so many moments to come. All I have is now.

Jesus, teach me to love, teach me to be present to the people you put in my life each day.

"Little children, let us not love in word or speech
but in deed and in truth." 1 John 3:18

"Now as they went on their way, he entered a village; and a woman
named Martha received him into her house. And she had a sister
called Mary, who sat at the Lord's feet and listened to his teaching.
But Martha was distracted with much serving; and she went to
him and said, 'Lord, do you not care that my sister has left me
to serve alone? Tell her then to help me.' But the Lord answered
her, 'Martha, Martha, you are anxious and troubled about many
things; one thing is needful. Mary has chosen the good portion,
which shall not be taken away from her." Luke 10:38-42

What are the consistent distractions that limit how well I love people when I am with them? What are the distractions that prevent me from success while I compete? How can I focus on the moment at hand on and off the field?

SEVENTY-SEVEN

Building Resolve

When I put in the time and see immediate results, it makes it much easier to work my tail off. The struggle often comes when I don't see those immediate results. I question my effort and the point of it all. Is it worth it? Will it even matter? I get anxious and begin to doubt.

I know in the end, that hard work, if directed properly, will be a blessing in my life. The grace that God gives me at every moment builds upon the effort I put forth in life. So in working hard at what I am called to do, I can trust that our Lord is taking that effort and multiplying it with his grace. When I pick hard work, I am directing my ability to choose in difficult moments. God will do astonishing things with that. He will strengthen my resolve.

Dear Lord, may my efforts increase every day. Help me to work hard and seek your glory in it.

"An athlete is not crowned unless he competes according to the rules. It is the hard-working farmer who ought to have the first share of the crops." 2 Timothy 2:5-6

"Look carefully then how you walk, not as unwise men but as wise, making the most of the time, because the days are evil. Therefore do not be foolish, but understand what the will of the Lord is." Ephesians 5:15-17

When am I tempted to laziness? When do I tend to work the hardest? How can I consistently remind myself to put forth a full effort for the Lord?

SEVENTY-EIGHT
Limiting Myself

Injury can severely limit what I can do physically. It becomes easy in those moments to focus on the things I can't do: can't run, can't lift, can't practice, can't compete, on and on and on. When I zone in on the "can't", I create a heavy burden upon my attitude and outlook in the situation. I miss an opportunity.

The better response to an injury is to focus on what I actually can do. If I am unable to change the things I can't do, I can at least fully run after the things I can. Perhaps more time in the film room, or encouraging teammates, or different forms of cardio, etc.

It is helpful to acknowledge my limitations, but not to focus on them and mope around. Do what I can, and do it well.

Jesus, when you hung from the cross, you didn't think about all the things you couldn't do. You thought about the amazing thing you were doing. Help me to have a similar outlook during the moments in my life I feel restricted and limited beyond my control. Make my thoughts and attitudes like yours.

"'he will wipe away every tear from their eyes, and death shall be no more, neither shall there be mourning nor crying nor pain any more, for the former things have passed away.' And he who sat upon the throne said, 'Behold, I make all things new...'" Revelation 21:4-5

"And David said to Saul, 'Let no man's heart fail because of him; your servant will go and fight with this Philistine.' And Saul said to David, 'You are not able to go against this Philistine to fight with him; for you are but a youth, and he has been a man of war from his youth.' But David said to Saul, 'Your servant used to keep sheep for his father; and when there came a lion, or a bear, and took a lamb from the flock, I went after him and smote him and delivered it out of his mouth; and if he arose against me, I caught him by his beard, and smote him and killed him. Your servant has killed both lions and bears; and this uncircumcised Philistine shall be like one of them, seeing he has defied the armies of the living God.'" 1 Samuel 17:32-36

Where am I focusing when I have an injury or setback – on what I can or can't do? What adjustments do I need to make to focus on what I can do and to utilize that opportunity to improve? How can I avoid limiting attitudes?

Integrity

Lots of people seem to be inconsistent in the way they live their life. I am one of those people. But, there are moments of hope.

I honestly do strive to tackle everything in my life with consistency, in athletics and beyond. I want my life to reflect one that is whole and deeply rooted in Christ. From the way I compete on the field to the way I spend time with friends off it, I hope there is never any doubt in the type of life I am trying to live. It is time to stop straddling the fence and living two lives. I need to be all in. I need to live my life with integrity.

Let there be no uncertainty in who I am and in what I stand for.

Sweet Jesus, by your grace may my life be one of integrity. May I direct all my thoughts, words and actions to serving you.

"He who walks in integrity walks securely, but he who perverts his ways will be found out." Proverbs 10:9

"Nothing is covered up that will not be revealed, or hidden that will not be known. Therefore whatever you have said in the dark shall be heard in the light, and what you have whispered in private rooms shall be proclaimed upon the housetops." Luke 12:2-3

When are the times I feel I am straddling the fence between the Christian life and the life of a non-believer? What is occurring in those moments? How can I change that?

Never Relent

I see three ways to respond when I fall: bounce up, stay down, or slowly lift myself up. The first and the last are worthy responses. The one in the middle is one I hope I never experience.

I can talk myself into almost anything. It is easy to convince myself to stay down if I find something to help me justify it. From what I can see, staying down is only good if a grizzly bear is on top of you, and you are playing dead. Why should I talk myself into staying down? What really justifies that action?

If Jesus stayed down any one of the three times he fell carrying his cross to be crucified, we would all be in a very bad place right now. I am invited by our Lord to follow and imitate him. Getting up has to be my only option, in life, in sports, in work, or in anything.

Lord, you never relented. Your desire to redeem us was such a driving force that nothing could get in your way. May I seek to glorify you with such a desire that I let nothing stop me.

"Now there is in Jerusalem by the Sheep Gate a pool, in Hebrew called Beth-zatha, which has five porticoes. In these lay a multitude of invalids, blind, lame, paralyzed. One man was there, who had been ill for thirty-eight years. When Jesus saw him and knew that he had been lying there a long time, he said to him, 'Do you want to be healed?' The sick man answered him, 'Sir, I have no man to put me into the pool when the water is troubled, and while I am going another steps down before me.' Jesus said to him, 'Rise, take up your pallet, and walk.'" John 5:2-8

What are the lines I tell myself to justify staying down? How can I switch that into positive talk? How can I make sure staying down is never an option?

When it fades

What is left when it all fades away? What happens when my career is over? I know it will end and much sooner than I hope. I am not sure what the experience will be like (or has been like). It is hard to imagine. I wonder if the end of my career will expose the reasons I played.

If my motivation to play is for myself, this ending will be difficult. The many ways I wrapped myself into this sport and everything associated with it will be gone. I will be left bare.

If I turn to the Lord, and make him the reason for my career, the transition will be different. It won't be as sad. It will actually be an exciting new adventure seeking his will. In that, I will find peace.

My purpose is to know the Lord and serve him.

Father, purify my heart. May I see my purpose in seeking your glory as your son or daughter.

"...Be strong and of good courage; be not frightened,
neither be dismayed; for the LORD your God
is with you wherever you go." Joshua 1:9

"Not that I have already obtained this or am already perfect; but
I press on to make it my own, because Christ Jesus has made me
his own. Brethren, I do not consider that I have made it my own;
but one thing I do, forgetting what lies behind and straining
forward to what lies ahead, I press on toward the goal for the prize
of the upward call of God in Christ Jesus." Philippians 3:12-14

What scares me the most about finishing my career? How can I change my outlook to become excited about the next chapter the Lord has planned for me? In what ways am I too attached to my athletic career?

My Idol

My body is quite impressive, both in what it is able to do and in how it looks. I mean, this is true for most athletes. We work hard for this; we sacrifice for this. I am rather amazed at what my body can achieve.

With all this, it can be easy, in a way, to idolize my body – to be obsessed with achieving its perfection or the fact that I already have. I start to treat it like a "god". I worship my body for my sake. I glory in my achievements and my appearance. This is folly. Idolizing my body removes the proper perspective on the wonder of God. I put the attention and accomplishment on me rather than his majesty.

God's word reminds me that my body is a temple of the Holy Spirit. God dwells within me – this is a great reason to treat my body well and with the proper emphasis. Not for my glory, but for his glory. And besides, my body is a gift. I did not create my arms or legs, or the ability to walk, etc. It came from him.

Lord, keep my eyes fixed on you. Let me proclaim words of gratitude all my days. Help me to respect my body's dignity all the while removing it from the pedestal on which I placed it.

"I appeal to you therefore, brethren, by the mercies of God, to present your bodies as a living sacrifice, holy and acceptable to God, which is your spiritual worship." Romans 12:1

"Do not be deceived; God is not mocked, for whatever a man sows, that he will also reap. For he who sows to his own flesh will from the flesh reap corruption; but he who sows to the Spirit will from the Spirit reap eternal life." Galatians 6:7-8

When do I find myself admiring my body and inflating my ego? How can I keep Christ at the center of my life and, in humility, recognize the gift he has given me in my body?

Proper Dependence

Don't drag the team down. Contribute. Nobody likes dead weight.

This attitude pervades the culture of athletics. It makes it hard for me to ask for help when I need it. I want to be someone that produces for the team. If we are as strong as the weakest link, I don't want to be that link.

In my relationship with the Lord, I carry this same attitude. Unfortunately, it should be the exact opposite. I need to be completely dependent upon him. He is the vine, and I am the branch. I can do nothing good apart from his grace.

Lord, humble me. May I never forget how dependent I am upon you.

> "Abide in me, and I in you. As the branch cannot bear fruit by itself, unless it abides in the vine, neither can you, unless you abide in me. I am the vine, you are the branches. He who abides in me, and I in him, he it is that bears much fruit, for apart from me you can do nothing." John 15:4-5

> "But if some of the branches were broken off, and you, a wild olive shoot, were grafted in their place to share the richness of the olive tree, do not boast over the branches. If you do boast, remember it is not you that support the root, but the root that supports you. You will say, 'Branches were broken off so that I might be grafted in.' That is true. They were broken off because of their unbelief, but you stand fast only through faith. So do not become proud, but stand in awe." Romans 11:17-20

In my Christian walk, where do I fail to recognize my deep dependence upon him? Why is it hard for me to depend upon God? Why is it hard for me to ask for help?

Passion

I would say most athletes, as I am, are passionate about their sport and their desire to succeed. I don't know why that passion isn't as prevalent in my relationship with God. I think of the abuse he took, the ridicule, the beatings, the betrayal, and I realize it was all for me.

I am willing to put my body on the line to win. Jesus did more than that for me. He not only did more, but he brought more intensity to our relationship. I can't imagine what it is like to hang from a cross and die. His love is so fervent for me, for all of us, that he did things I will never fully understand until heaven.

God is passionately in love with me. I hope I can love him one day with a similar passion.

Lord, you gave me such a desire to compete – grow a similar desire in my heart for you.

> "And it was the third hour, when they crucified him. And the inscription of the charge against him read, 'The King of the Jews.' And with him they crucified two robbers, one on his right and one on his left. And those who passed by derided him, wagging their heads, and saying, 'Aha! You who would destroy the temple and build it in three days, save yourself, and come down from the cross!' So also the chief priests mocked him to one another with the scribes, saying, 'He saved others; he cannot save himself. Let the Christ, the King of Israel, come down now from the cross, that we may see and believe.' Those who were crucified with him also reviled him." Mark 15:25-32

What creates a strong passion in my heart? Why is this lacking in my love for God? How can I try to fix this?

Going for Greatness

Go big…or go little. Do I strive to be great because it is the better way, or do I let fear, apathy, or laziness reduce me to shallow achievements?

I wasn't made to settle. The Lord didn't make me for this mediocrity, nor does my soul desire it. I was made to reach the heights of greatness. If my motivation, in the moment, is to reach this height, then I am in a good place. I should carry on.

If I find myself constantly dodging the potential greatness before me, I need help. I need to turn this attitude of mine on its head. I need to strive for the great things because they are great. I need to punt the mediocrity.

Lord, give me a spirit that desires greatness in all things because this is the superior way. May I embrace this way of life and come to know the fullness of what you intend for me.

"In a great house there are not only vessels of gold and silver but also of wood and earthenware, and some for noble use, some for ignoble. If any one purifies himself from what is ignoble, then he will be a vessel for noble use, consecrated and useful to the master of the house, ready for any good work. So shun youthful passions and aim at righteousness, faith, love, and peace, along with those who call upon the Lord from a pure heart. Have nothing to do with stupid, senseless controversies; you know that they breed quarrels. And the Lord's servant must not be quarrelsome but kindly to every one, an apt teacher, forbearing, correcting his opponents with gentleness. God may perhaps grant that they will repent and come to know the truth, and they may escape from the snare of the devil, after being captured by him to do his will." 2 Timothy 2:20-26

In what ways can I improve my pursuit of greatness in life? When do I back down from an opportunity to do something great? What is my most frequent hindrance – laziness, fear, etc.?

Being a Friend

I have my eyes set on the goal. No one can get in my way. Actually, a lot of people seem to get in my way. Or maybe that is just my perspective. I need people in my life, but I need to stop using and abusing them. I have a tendency to buddy up to people when I need something – to reach my goals. If that same person then gets in the way of my goals, I am gone.

In other words, I use people a lot. Sometimes they are my friends. In these moments, I am not being a good friend in return. I am actually not being one at all. It is much easier to be selfish than it is to be gracious and caring. My soul was not made for the easy way; it was made for the road less traveled.

To be a real friend is to walk the road of discipleship together, or at least to walk the road of virtue together. This means caring for the person, hoping and encouraging them to constantly grow. It means loving them and wanting them to reach their potential.

Lord, forgive all the ways I use my friends. Give me the grace to serve them. Help me to put myself second.

"Two are better than one, because they have a good reward
for their toil. For if they fall, one will lift up his fellow; but
woe to him who is alone when he falls and has not another
to lift him up. Again, if two lie together, they are warm;
but how can one be warm alone? And though a man might
prevail against one who is alone, two will withstand him. A
threefold cord is not quickly broken." Ecclesiastes 4:9-12

"A friend loves at all times, and a brother is
born for adversity." Proverbs 17:17

"and let us consider how to stir up one another to love and
good works, not neglecting to meet together, as is the habit
of some, but encouraging one another, and all the more
as you see the Day drawing near." Hebrews 10:24-25

Who do I tend to "use" the most? How can I invest better into these relationships? Who stirs me up to love and good works? Who do I inspire to live this way?

Calm

Overreacting followed by regret is a scenario that gets old.

It is remarkable how being calm helps maintain peace in my heart. That peace flows out into other areas of my life. To stop and recognize my feelings of anger, yet be able to think through the proper reaction is such a gift. I am thankful for the ability to be meek. I am thankful for the ability to play out a different scenario.

I am clear headed; I am kind; I am enjoyable to be around – at all times. I am grateful I have control over my anger and can turn it into strength. I am grateful I can remain calm and not overreact.

Jesus, increase my meekness. May I be more like you.

"A man without self-control is like a city broken
into and left without walls." Proverbs 25:28

"Know this, my beloved brethren. Let every man be quick
to hear, slow to speak, slow to anger, for the anger of
man does not work the righteousness of God. Therefore
put away all filthiness and rank growth of wickedness
and receive with meekness the implanted word, which is
able to save your souls. But be doers of the word, and not
hearers only, deceiving yourselves." James 1:19-22

What am I like when I control my anger? How do I feel when I am meek? How does it affect those around me when I am able to be calm?

My Response

There are plenty of moments in my life when I need to say "no". Moments when the activity is not good for me, physically or spiritually. Moments when the conversation or environment is not good for me. At times, these moments could jeopardize my playing time or my social status. How will I respond?

It takes courage to say "no". It takes courage to face a particular fear and act directly contrary to it: the fear of being different, of ridicule, of missing out, or any other fear. I need to prevent it from controlling me. I can't let fear paralyze me and thus float down stream like a dead fish.

Dear Lord, give me the courage to see through the temptation and choose the right path. Allow me the grace to say "no" when I need to.

"No temptation has overtaken you that is not common to man. God is faithful, and he will not let you be tempted beyond your strength, but with the temptation will also provide the way of escape, that you may be able to endure it." 1 Corinthians 10:13

"Finally, be strong in the Lord and in the strength of his might. Put on the whole armor of God, that you may be able to stand against the wiles of the devil. For we are not contending against flesh and blood, but against the principalities, against the powers, against the world rulers of this present darkness, against the spiritual hosts of wickedness in the heavenly places. Therefore take the whole armor of God, that you may be able to withstand in the evil day, and having done all, to stand." Ephesians 6:10-13

What are some scenarios that require me to say "no"? When am I most likely to give in and say "yes"? How can I change that?

Beyond the Feelings

When I train hard, I like to see results. I think that is relatively common among athletes. We like goals, results, and other tangible things.

With my faith, it sometimes is less tangible. If I pray, go to church, and get involved in other activities, I eventually get to that point when I feel like I don't get out of it what I am putting into it. Jesus spoke about this in a parable. He said some seeds fall on rocky ground and spring up fast but have no roots. So when things get tough, it withers and dies (see Matthew 13:3-9).

I want to continue to grow in my faith when it doesn't feel as fun or exciting. I need to remember that faith is hard to quantify. If I am becoming a better person, then my faith is growing. Praise God.

Lord, by your grace keep me faithful till the day of my death. Help me not rely on what I feel. Instead, increase my faith so that nothing may shake me.

> "If we endure, we shall also reign with him; if we
> deny him, he also will deny us;" 2 Timothy 2:12

> "Let us hold fast the confession of our hope without wavering,
> for he who promised is faithful;" Hebrews 10:23

Does the way I feel often dictate what I do and think? How can I break free of that cycle? What can I do to avoid unplugging from my faith life when I don't *feel* as excited about it?

NINETY

My All

Why am I not willing to sacrifice? It is like I turn my back to the Lord and just walk on to the beat of my own drum. That wouldn't work on my team. Why do I let it into other areas of my life – especially my relationship with God? When I give, I too often count the cost.

No more. It is time to give the Lord my everything. Take all of me Lord – my pride, my desires, my loves, my addictions, my social life, my free time, my playing time, my practices, my popularity, my heart, and my sexuality.

Take it all Lord. It is only then that I will find life.

"In all things I have shown you that by so toiling one must help
the weak, remembering the words of the Lord Jesus, how he
said, 'It is more blessed to give than to receive.'" Acts 20:35

"The point is this: he who sows sparingly will also
reap sparingly, and he who sows bountifully will
also reap bountifully." 2 Corinthians 9:6

What am I holding back from the Lord – a relationship, a sin, a habit, a vice? How can I give everything to the Lord starting now? Who can help me in this?

Spending Time

Gratitude, identity, responsibility, leadership, service, role models – there are so many different topics to inspire me to create a better world. I have been given so much in my talents and my faith. To keep all of these gifts to myself would be a great act of selfishness. Instead, I must look outward. To follow Jesus is to participate in his mission of salvation. He asks me to contribute in the work of evangelization, of sharing the good news. In fact, I have a mandate from Jesus himself. In my baptism, I am called to be an apostle. I am a priest, prophet and king. I am a follower of Jesus.

Of all the ways I could spend my time, what could be better than spending it in line with Jesus' mission? Nothing. To help change a life and give someone the chance to spend eternity in heaven rather than hell is a pretty big deal. It is such a big deal that it is worth any amount of sacrifice for one soul to get to heaven.

Lord, help me to share my story. Help me to inspire others by my journey of faith. Give me the courage and trust to be an evangelist, with great love.

> "…Always be prepared to make a defense to any one
> who calls you to account for the hope that is in you, yet
> do it with gentleness and reverence." 1 Peter 3:15

> "What man of you, having a hundred sheep, if he has lost one
> of them, does not leave the ninety-nine in the wilderness, and
> go after the one which is lost, until he finds it? And when he
> has found it, he lays it on his shoulders, rejoicing. And when
> he comes home, he calls together his friends and his neighbors,
> saying to them, 'Rejoice with me, for I have found my sheep
> which was lost.' Just so, I tell you, there will be more joy in
> heaven over one sinner who repents than over ninety-nine
> righteous persons who need no repentance." Luke 15:4-7

Who has God put in my life? Of those individuals, does the Lord want me to share his story with them? Can I start praying for those individuals by name?

Standing Alone

Sometimes leaders are left standing alone. I have to be willing to put my neck on the line and risk being isolated. In a team environment, it is hard to be alone, apart from my teammates. Unfortunately, there may come a time when I need to be.

While I may still be learning what it means, I desire to have Jesus at the center of my life. I realize standing apart from the crowd might be necessary, even if it means being ostracized by them. The good thing is, I am actually never alone. If I aspire to stand for him, even if no one else will, he will always be right there with me.

Heavenly Father, your goodness is without limit. Remind me that standing up for your honor and glory is necessary at times. Give me the grace to do it, even if I am the only one.

> "fear not, for I am with you, be not dismayed, for I am
> your God; I will strengthen you, I will help you, I will
> uphold you with my victorious right hand." Isaiah 41:10

> "But before all this they will lay their hands on you and persecute
> you, delivering you up to the synagogues and prisons, and you
> will be brought before kings and governors for my name's sake.
> This will be a time for you to bear testimony." Luke 21:12-13

When have I failed to stand apart from the crowd for the sake of Jesus? Why am I afraid to stand alone for him?

Surrender

When things in my life tank, it is really hard not to interrogate God. "Why" is a question that I ask a lot. It is difficult to understand why he lets things happen that are so tough. I think sometimes I look at God like a sugar daddy, or a Santa Claus – give me what I want, when I want it, and if you don't, I get perturbed. I understand it is ok to pray for a win, a start, or a record, but in the end I need to surrender to his will for me and to trust that it is the better option.

Jesus was hanging from the cross in what seemed like utter failure. Before he yielded up his spirit, he cried out, "My God, my God, why have you forsaken me?" (see Matthew 27:46). The drama seems to be so thick. He is hanging, being murdered by the Romans, and crying out in what seems like despair. Yet, he is God and incapable of despair. He was actually quoting Psalm 22. He was saying to me, "I understand you will experience difficult moments in life that seem as if I have abandoned you. But I never will." The second half of Psalm 22 turns from a cry of help to a song of praise. It reminds me that God is always near me, helping me, calling to me, and seeking to do what is best for me in his providential care.

In my dark hours of failure, or suffering, or loss, or whatever it may be, I need to surrender it to the Lord and trust myself to his care.

Dear Jesus, life can be hard. Give me a strong spirit of hope. Remind me to lay my concerns at the foot of your cross.

> "But I trust in you, O LORD, I say, 'You are my God.'
> My times are in your hand; deliver me from the hand of
> my enemies and persecutors! Let your face shine on your
> servant; save me in your merciful love!" Psalm 31:14-16

> "I consider that the sufferings of this present
> time are not worth comparing with the glory
> that is to be revealed to us." Romans 8:18

When do I question the goodness of God? How can I begin to treat God as my Father instead of just my provider?

Always Giving

If I stop extending beyond myself, I will suffocate my own flourishing. Like the Dead Sea that has no water flowing out from it and no life within it, when I am not giving, I risk death – a spiritual death. With faith, the only way to ensure keeping it is to give it to others. It is seemingly a paradox – if I don't share it, I will likely fail to keep it.

God is Father, Son and Holy Spirit – a communion of Divine Persons, constantly making a complete gift of one to the other. He is a communion of love. When I give, I imitate him and am made more complete. The giving stirs a deeper spiritual life inside my soul. I lessen the risk of death by living in imitation of the giver of all life – God.

When I fail to give, I risk losing life within me. I risk becoming like the Dead Sea.

Holy Trinity, three persons, one God, give me the grace to give and not count the cost. Create in me a constant stream of pure giving.

"In all things I have shown you that by so toiling one must help the weak, remembering the words of the Lord Jesus, how he said, 'It is more blessed to give than to receive.'" Acts 20:35

"One man gives freely, yet grows all the richer; another withholds what he should give, and only suffers want." Proverbs 11:24

When is it hardest for me to give? What is the most difficult thing for me to give to another? Why is it hard for me to give?

Indifference

I put 100% into it, full throttle. Whether it is my sport, workouts, school, or work, I go all the way. When I stop caring this much, the outcome starts to suffer. I have seen this; I know this.

In my relationship with God, I often don't go at it with the same intensity. The time, the sacrifices, the effort – it just isn't at the same level with my faith. I struggle with indifference towards God. I am a mediocre disciple. With the most important thing I will ever deal with in my life, I go at it half way. Why?

Jesus is the way, the truth, and the life; he is the source of joy and happiness. Indifference towards this is a serious burden to flourishing. It will create a shallow existence, and in the end will lead to a frustrating life.

My Lord and my God, heal me of this indifference. Burn in my heart an overwhelming desire for you.

> "I know your works: you are neither cold nor hot. Would that you were cold or hot! So, because you are lukewarm, and neither cold nor hot, I will spew you out of my mouth." Revelation 3:15-16

> "To another he said, 'Follow me.' But he said, 'Lord, let me first go and bury my father.' But he said to him, 'Leave the dead to bury their own dead; but as for you, go and proclaim the kingdom of God.' Another said, 'I will follow you, Lord; but let me first say farewell to those at my home.' Jesus said to him, 'No one who puts his hand to the plow and looks back is fit for the kingdom of God.'" Luke 9:59-62

Why don't I put much effort into my relationship with Christ? How can I fight the attitude of indifference with Jesus? What is the excuse I tell myself?

Faithful Witnesses

To be a role model is often times to be different. It is swimming upstream when everyone else is riding down the current. It takes commitment, courage, and prudence.

Role models are tremendous assets to society. Every saint provides us with a tangible, human role model, who by God's grace lived a life worthy of imitation. If I want to be a role model, reading their lives will be a valuable use of my time. It will be good to fill my mind with stories of what it looks like to give all to Jesus, and to inspire others to do the very same thing.

I don't need to re-create the wheel. The more I read and fill my mind with stories of lives well lived, the more it will become part of who I am. It will influence me. This is what I want. That is what I need. Their stories will teach me how be like Jesus and to have a lasting impact for him.

Father of mercy, you have poured your grace out upon humanity and, in your goodness, raised up leaders among your people to be witness for us to admire. Make their stories draw me closer to you.

"What you have learned and received and heard and seen in me, do; and the God of peace will be with you." Philippians 4:9

"So I exhort the elders among you, as a fellow elder and a witness of the sufferings of Christ as well as a partaker in the glory that is to be revealed. Tend the flock of God that is your charge, not by constraint but willingly, not for shameful gain but eagerly, not as domineering over those in your charge but being examples to the flock. And when the chief Shepherd is manifested you will obtain the unfading crown of glory. Likewise you that are younger be subject to the elders..." 1 Peter 5:1-5

Who is someone I can learn from that has been a faithful follower of Jesus? What is my hesitation in picking up a book like this? Why is filling my mind with these types of stories powerful for my own growth?

NINETY-SEVEN

Following Rules

Following Jesus means following a lot a rules. There are a plethora of "don'ts" in the Christian life. I am guilty of focusing on this and rebelling against it.

Yes, there are a lot of rules. But, rather than complaining, I need to discover why they exist. In my sport, if you take away the rules, you have no sport. You instead have chaos. The fun is gone. The game is lost and so is the freedom.

When our Lord gives me rules, it is similar to sports. He is guiding my life so that I can exist in a good and healthy relationship with him. If you take away the rules, I will have chaos in life. I will no longer know what it means to be a child of God, a disciple of Jesus, or a friend to my neighbor. He made me, hence he knows how I thrive.

Following the "don'ts" of Jesus allows me to fully embrace the "do's". With this, I will know life and have it to its fullest.

Lord, change my attitude. Help me to focus on our relationship and what will help it flourish. Help me to understand the great good that your rules provide me.

> "But the fruit of the Spirit is love, joy, peace,
> patience, kindness, goodness, faithfulness,
> gentleness, self-control..." Galatians 5:22-23

> "As the Father has loved me, so have I loved you; abide in my
> love. If you keep my commandments, you will abide in my
> love, just as I have kept my Father's commandments and abide
> in his love. These things I have spoken to you, that my joy
> may be in you, and that your joy may be full." John 15:9-11

What is blocking my understanding that these rules are meant to help my relationship with God flourish? What rules do I focus on with the most negativity? How can I discover how that rule aids my relationship with God?

Ridicule for Jesus

Ridicule is not foreign to me as an athlete. Getting booed and yelled at is all part of the game. I keep my eye on the prize, and let this stuff bounce off me.

Ridicule is also part of following Jesus. He was treated worse than I will likely ever know. Why should I be any different? If he didn't preserve himself from this conduct, why should I be spared it? I am more than happy to take a few jabs for Jesus. Bring it.

The only sad part is the people delivering the punches don't understand that Jesus is everything. They haven't yet met him. Maybe I can offer up the experience of being ridiculed for them. Responding with love might play a part in helping them encounter him.

Jesus, you became one of us knowing you would be rejected. Help me to never be dissuaded from doing the right thing because of the fear of being ridiculed.

"Blessed are you when men revile you and persecute you and utter all kinds of evil against you falsely on my account. Rejoice and be glad, for your reward is great in heaven, for so men persecuted the prophets who were before you." Matthew 5:11-12

"Now you have observed my teaching, my conduct, my aim in life, my faith, my patience, my love, my steadfastness, my persecutions, my sufferings, what befell me at Antioch, at Iconium, and at Lystra, what persecutions I endured; yet from them all the Lord rescued me. Indeed all who desire to live a godly life in Christ Jesus will be persecuted, while evil men and impostors will go on from bad to worse, deceivers and deceived." 2 Timothy 3:10-13

When am I most vulnerable to fearing ridicule? What should my reactions be? How can I be a courageous witness when I suspect ridicule will come my way?

Small "Souledness"

When I have an opportunity in front of me to reach for greatness, and I fail to try, a sadness comes over me. It is like my soul knows I wasn't made to settle or turn from opportunities like that. In sports, they come along often enough. The trick is to be motivated by the call for greatness rather than my own desire for glory.

In life, the opportunities to be magnanimous are also plentiful. Do I stop and talk to the homeless person, or just avoid eye contact? Do I go on the mission trip, or just make excuses that make me sound more important than I really am? Do I take the job that will be a challenge but a noble calling, or am I comfortable doing what I am doing?

When I fail to reach for heights that are worthy, noble and within my ability, sadness touches my soul. Mediocrity, fear, and laziness are all stifling. I need to look into the face of God and seek his will on a daily basis. I need to answer his call to become a son or daughter worthy of imitation. I need to grow in magnanimity, or greatness of soul.

Lord, may your passion, death and resurrection be a constant motivation for me to use the gifts I have been given and to strive for greatness.

> "And behold, one came up to him, saying, 'Teacher, what good deed must I do, to have eternal life?' And he said to him, 'Why do you ask me about what is good? One there is who is good. If you would enter life, keep the commandments.' He said to him, 'Which?' And Jesus said, 'You shall not kill, You shall not commit adultery, You shall not steal, You shall not bear false witness, Honor your father and mother, and, You shall love your neighbor as yourself.' The young man said to him, 'All these I have observed; what do I still lack?' Jesus said to him, 'If you would be perfect, go, sell what you possess and give to the poor, and you will have treasure in heaven; and come, follow me.' When the young man heard this he went away sorrowful; for he had great possessions." Matthew 19:16-22

When do I settle for small things? How does this settling affect me? What changes in my life should I make to avoid the sadness similar to the sadness of the rich young man?

A Daily Choice

There are a lot of reflections in this book. Some of the themes are closely related. Some have hit me more than others. What I know is that living as a Christian athlete means choosing *every* day.

I must choose to wake up, to train, to study, to serve the Lord, to do the things that are most conducive to my spiritual health and to reject the things that will damage it.

I have been blessed in this life. Not every day will be easy or even make sense. If I fight with all my effort to choose Christ and persevere through this journey of life, I should be in a good place at the end. His faithfulness will help me in the tough moments. His grace will sustain me.

Dear Lord, I choose to serve you. May your grace strengthen me in this choice.

> "Now therefore fear the LORD, and serve him in sincerity and in faithfulness; put away the gods which your fathers served beyond the River, and in Egypt, and serve the LORD. And if you be unwilling to serve the LORD, choose this day whom you will serve, whether the gods your fathers served in the region beyond the River, or the gods of the Amorites in whose land you dwell; but as for me and my house, we will serve the LORD." Joshua 24:14-15

> "Behold, I stand at the door and knock; if any one hears my voice and opens the door, I will come in to him and eat with him, and he with me." Revelation 3:20

When do I fail to choose the Lord? What do I choose instead of him? Who can help me make better choices and hold me accountable to them? What words can I say at the beginning of each day to let the Lord know I choose him?

ACKNOWLEDGEMENTS

I would like to thank Sarah O'Brien, my editor, for her hard work on this project. I can't thank enough Mike Sweeney for his love and encouragement over the years and the contribution he has made to this manuscript. Amazing Mike!

Heartfelt gratitude to all my colleagues in FOCUS for their fraternal love and support, especially Curtis for getting the whole thing started and being God's faithful instrument.

I want to thank the missionaries that serve on campus with the remarkable student-athletes that are desiring to grow into spectacular souls. They are the ones who are making a difference in countless lives.

I am grateful for my parents and siblings. It is so valuable knowing you are loved.

Of course, a very special thank you to my wife, Kate, for her patience, support and encouragement in this long process. I am grateful for her belief in this and the sacrifices she has made to allow this project to come to completion.

Lastly, I am grateful for the gift of faith in my life given by God, who is love and mercy.

INDEX OF REFLECTION THEMES

ABOUT THE AUTHOR

Thomas has been around sports his entire life. He was an all-state quarterback in high school, helping his team to the state finals in Arizona. He went to the University of San Diego on a Presidential Scholarship and played a season of football. He finished his last three years of undergraduate work at Benedictine College and played club level rugby. While completing his Bachelor's degree, he had a profound encounter with the Lord in large part through those he met involved with the Fellowship of Catholic University Students (FOCUS). He has worked with college athletes since 2001 as a missionary with FOCUS. He launched Varsity Catholic, a division within FOCUS that serves the faith needs of student-athletes across the country. He received his Master's degree in Catechetics and Evangelization as a member of the first graduating class of the Augustine Institute. His website is www.faithandathletics.com, and has been featured on the Catholic Church's Pontifical Council for the Laity, Church and Sport section's website.

He strongly believes in the significant role sports can play in developing men and women of exceptional faith and character.

He resides in Littleton, CO with his wife and children.

You can connect with him at the following:
Twitter: www.twitter.com/twurtz13
Linkedin: www.linkedin.com/in/twurtz13

ABOUT VARSITY CATHOLIC

In 2007, Varsity Catholic was launched as a division of FOCUS, the Fellowship of Catholic University Students. While serving as a FOCUS missionary, Thomas Wurtz, the founding director of Varsity Catholic, recognized the unique needs and challenges student-athletes face, as sometimes their status, time, and/or energy doesn't allow them an easy opportunity to invest in their spiritual growth. Responding to this challenge, FOCUS launched Varsity Catholic to provide student-athletes with comprehensive development during their collegiate experience and addresses the challenges these athletes face keeping their faith alive.

With this desire to serve the formative needs of student-athletes, Varsity Catholic staff seek to have a consistent presence, always wanting to be available for the athletes. They offer students an opportunity to learn how to live as Christian athletes on the college campus. Visit www.varsitycatholic.org for more information.

ABOUT FOCUS

Recognizing the dire need for Catholic campus outreach, and inspired by Pope John Paul II's call to a "new evangelization", Curtis Martin and his wife, Michaelann founded FOCUS, the Fellowship of Catholic University Students, in 1998 at Benedictine College in Atchison, Kansas.

FOCUS invites college students into a growing relationship with Jesus Christ and His Church, inspiring and equipping them for a lifetime of Christ-centered evangelization, discipleship and friendships in which they lead others to do the same. During the 2014-2015 academic year, 434 missionaries are serving full-time on 100 college campuses in 34 states. As of the fall of 2014, more than 13,000 FOCUS staff and student alumni are involved with parishes throughout the US. Within this number, 495 have made decisions to pursue Catholic religious vocations. For more information, visit www.focus.org.

NOTES

NOTES

NOTES

NOTES

NOTES

NOTES